The Pioneer Cookbook

The Pioneer Cookbook
Recipes for Today's Kitchen

Miriam Barton

LEATHERWOOD
PRESS

For Jeremy, Eliza, and Mikey—as always.

Cover recipes: buttermilk biscuits (page 118) and strawberry preserves (page 167)

Leatherwood Press, LLC
110 South 800 West
Brigham City, Utah 84302

ISBN: 978-1-59992-142-6

Use caution when following the recipes and methods in this book. The author and publisher will not be held
responsible for any adverse affect that may arise from the use of these recipes and methods.

Table of Contents

Acknowledgements

I would like to thank the team at Walnut Springs Press for giving me the opportunity to write this pioneer cookbook and have it published. Thank you to Sue Larson, a fabulous friend and neighbor, for your help. Special thanks to my husband for his constant support and encouragement, as well as my children for being great sports about the dividing of my time as I wrote this book. Above all, I want to express gratitude to my Heavenly Father for all of His blessings in my life and for preserving and bringing my ancestors to this great land so long ago.

Introduction

It has been many, many years since pioneers settled the great American frontier. The pioneers were a strong and sturdy breed; they had to be. Every day was filled with hard labor, and the pioneers had to possess an inner determination in order to survive and to make a better life for themselves and their descendants.

The pioneers came from every nationality and walk of life, seeking wealth, religious freedom, or simply a plot of land they could call their own. They traveled by boat, train, horse- or oxen-drawn wagons, and on foot while pushing handcarts. The harshness of the journey did not keep these good people from making their mark on United States civilization and history.

The pioneers were industrious and ambitious people. Once they reached their desired destination they made settlements, built their own houses, and plowed the land. They shared with their neighbors and helped one another. They made do with whatever was available. When they cooked, if they were missing certain ingredients, they would simply change up the recipe and invent new cuisine. They ate very simply but heartily.

I hope this pioneer cookbook becomes a treasured reference in your home. The recipes are simple and tasty. Though these recipes have been adapted for modern kitchens, perhaps the taste and ingredients will remind you of days gone by, when food was cooked over an open fire and everything was made from scratch.

How the Pioneers Cooked

Pioneers prepared very hearty and simple foods out of necessity. Their means of cooking were equally simple. Typically, they used equipment such as Dutch ovens, frying pans, boiling pots, and roasting spits. Simple stoves could be purchased and brick ovens built once a home was secured.

Dutch ovens are cooking pots that have thick walls and tight-fitting lids so as to create an oven-type effect for the food cooking inside a pot. During the late seventeenth century, the Dutch began producing these portable ovens using an advanced method of metal casting; hence, the name Dutch oven. An Englishman named Abraham Darby spent four years in the Netherlands observing the making of these lidded pots with dry sand, then returned home to England and started making similar pots. Also, Dutch traders would go from door to door and sell these pots, which were so valuable that they were often included in the properties given out in wills when a person died. After the Dutch oven reached the British colonies in America, legs were added to the pot in order to place it above the coals of a fire. Dutch ovens were used for every kind of cooking: baking, frying, boiling, stewing, and roasting. They could be used over open fires, under hot coals from fires, in an oven, or on a stove, proving themselves very versatile. When pioneers traveled, a Dutch oven could be found hanging from the wagon; it went everywhere the pioneers went. The Dutch oven has been used for hundreds of years and is still popular today. Of course, Dutch ovens have changed over the years. At the present time, they are commonly ceramic or aluminum instead of iron, and they are often coated with enamel and come in different colors. However used over the centuries, the concept of cooking in a pot that is like an oven remains the same, and Dutch ovens have withstood the test of time.

A wood-burning stove is just that, a metal (usually iron or steel) stove that is heated by wood as fuel. These stoves are connected to chimneys for gases to escape, and they feature adjustable air controls. Around 1800, Count Rumford of England invented the cooking stove. It was very large, designed for enormous working kitchens, such as in castles. Stewart Oberlin came up with a compact stove for a regular house in the year 1834. The cook stove evolved through time. Soon after the wood stove came the coal and kerosene stove, then eventually gas, and finally electric in the late 1800s (though it wasn't available for widespread use until the mid-1900s). Stoves have indeed changed through time, and we can assume that most everyone would choose to cook over a stove if the other option was building and cooking over fires three times a day. Thank heaven for that invention!

Most pioneers used fire—whether in a fireplace or out of doors—to cook and heat their food. And just as in our day, they had all kinds of gadgets to make cooking as convenient as possible. They used muffin tins that would fully enclose the batter so they could be placed in or near the fire. Waffle irons employed the same concept. Pioneers had fireplace "cranes" that would hold hanging pots over the fire. Some people even had "toasters"—long-handled metal clamps for holding slices of bread near the fire until the bread was perfectly browned. Of course, there were other kitchen gadgets, such as butter churners, baskets used to separate curd from whey to make cheese, and pie safes, which protected pies from insects and rodents. In addition, there were hand-crank appliances like meat grinders, juicers, and grain mills.

The pioneers worked hard for everything they had and ate. They were also very industrious at coming up with handy tools around the kitchen—tools that did not require electricity.
Some things were unavoidable, however, such as lye soap, which was made from water, ashes, and lard. The pioneers used lye soap for everything—bathing, washing dishes, scrubbing floors, and laundering clothing and bedding. As far as hygiene goes, most pioneers on the trail would wash their dishes and bathe in creeks and streams. When a homestead was secured and the family set up a small bathtub (a very large bucket), baths were only taken once a week, if that, and the same bath water was shared by all. The oldest in the family would get to bathe first and they would continue on down the line until the baby was washed. (As you can imagine, the water was very dirty by the time the baby was washed; that's where the phrase "throw the baby out with the bath water" came from.) Times were very certainly different then than they are today.

Main Dishes

The Pioneer Woman

Grandmother, on a winter's day,
Milked the cows and fed them hay;
Slopped the hogs, harnessed the mule,
And got the children off to school.

Did a washing, mopped the floors,
Washed the windows and did some
   chores,
Cooked a dish of home-dried fruit,
And pressed her husband's Sunday suit.

Swept the parlor, made the beds,
Baked a dozen loaves of bread,
Split the firewood, lugged some in,
Enough to fill the kitchen bin.

Churned the butter, baked a cake,
And then exclaimed, "For goodness
   sake,
Those darned calves are out again!"
Went and chased them into the pen.

Gathered the eggs, locked the stable,
Back to the house to set the table;

Cooked a supper that was delicious,
Afterward washed up all the dishes.

Fed the animals, sprinkled the clothes,
Mended a basket full of hose,
Then opened the organ and began to
   play
"When You Come to the End of a Perfect
   Day"!

AUTHOR UNKNOWN

→BARBECUED BRISKET←

Visit any respectable barbecue in Texas and you will almost always find brisket as the main course. A brisket is half of the pectoral muscle of a steer, taken from between the forelegs. It is a hard-worked muscle but can be very tender if cooked properly. A brisket can be cooked in the oven, in a smoker, or on a grill. (If grilling or smoking the brisket, you may omit the liquid smoke.) "Barbeque" actually means cooking meat slowly over charcoal or wood, so keep that in mind if you want the meal to be authentic. That said, my grandmother, a Texan, always baked her brisket, and it was the best I ever tasted. Everyone else I know smokes the brisket. Brisket is commonly served with potato salad (see page 92), baked beans (see page 94), and cornbread (see page 116).

5-pound brisket
1 teaspoon salt
½ cup ketchup
2 tablespoons apple cider vinegar
2 tablespoons brown sugar
1 Worcestershire sauce
1½ teaspoons liquid smoke
¼ teaspoon pepper
½ cup chopped onion
1 bay leaf

Heat oven to 325°F. Rub the surface of the brisket with salt. Place in an ungreased rectangular baking dish.

In a separate bowl, mix remaining ingredients, then spread over the brisket.

Cover with foil and bake for about 3 hours, occasionally basting the brisket with the drippings. Remove from oven when meat is done according to taste (medium-well, well-done, etc.). If desired, serve the brisket with the pan juices and/or barbeque sauce.

☞ *Kissin' wears out, cookin' don't.*

→ROAST BEEF←

Roast beef was brought to America by English immigrants. It is traditionally served as Sunday dinner, with the leftovers enjoyed throughout the week in between slices of bread.

6- to 7-pound beef rib or loin roast
¼ cup butter, melted
1 teaspoon salt
¼ teaspoon pepper
1 tablespoon flour

Heat the oven to 350ºF. Place the beef on a dripping pan.

In a small bowl, stir together the butter, salt, and pepper. Baste the beef with this mixture.

Bake the roast for 2 to 2½ hours, basting it with the drippings and any remaining butter mixture every 30 minutes.

Skim the fat drippings and whisk them together with flour. Bring to a boil in a small saucepan. Serve on the side as gravy.

→MEATLOAF←

Meatloaf is a traditional German, Belgian, and Dutch dish. It is also a cousin to the Italian meatball. The American-style meatloaf we love today comes from the German-Americans who lived in colonial Pennsylvania.

1½ pounds ground beef
1 cup milk
1 tablespoon Worcestershire sauce
1 egg
3 slices of bread, torn into small
    pieces
¼ cup chopped onion
1 garlic clove, minced
½ teaspoon salt
½ teaspoon garlic salt
½ teaspoon pepper
½ teaspoon mustard
½ cup ketchup
1 tablespoon brown sugar
1 teaspoon ground nutmeg

Preheat oven to 350ºF. In a mixing bowl, combine all ingredients except the ketchup, brown sugar, and nutmeg. Make sure the mixture is well combined (using your hands is the most effective method), then spread the meat mixture in an 8-inch square baking dish.

In a separate bowl, mix together the ketchup, brown sugar, and nutmeg. Spread the ketchup sauce evenly over the raw meat.

Bake for 1 hour and 15 minutes. Make sure the meat is completely cooked in the center before removing from the oven.

Let cool for at least 5 minutes before serving.

⇥HODGEPOT⇤

This recipe came from Dutch settlers. The meat and vegetables were cooked together, and then the vegetables were removed and mashed.

> 3- to 4-pound pot roast or beef steak
> 6 to 8 cups water
> 3 teaspoons salt
> 1½ pounds potatoes, peeled and
>   quartered
> 3 carrots, cut into large slices
> 1 large onion, chopped

> 3 tablespoons water
> ½ cup milk
> 3 tablespoons flour

Sear the beef on each side in a large soup pot or slow cooker. Place the vegetables and salt in the pot with the beef.

Cover and cook on medium to medium-high heat until the meat and vegetables are very tender (if using a slow cooker, cook on high).

Remove the vegetables, place them in a large mixing bowl, and mash them together with the water, milk, and flour. Serve the mashed vegetables on the side of the meat.

☞ *Them that works hard eats hardy.*

⇥CORNED BEEF⇤

This is a primitive recipe that requires a small barrel to replicate the pioneers' method of corning beef. Corned beef, properly stored, can be preserved for up to two months, making it very valuable to pioneers as food storage, particularly in the winter.

> beef quarter, cut into roasting pieces
> 3 pounds brown sugar
> ½ pound saltpeter
> ½ cup baking soda
> 2 tablespoons crushed red pepper

Pack the beef closely in a barrel.

Dissolve the remaining ingredients in about 4 gallons of water, then pour the mixture over the packed beef (make sure the beef is fully covered; if it is not, you will need to add more water). Store the barrel in a very cool place for about a week.

Pour the brine into large pots and boil it, then skim off the blood and pour the brine back onto the beef.

The corned beef is now ready to be stored (in the brine) for up to 2 months. Can be served hot or cold.

⇥TRADITIONAL SHEPHERD'S PIE⇤

The English have eaten meat pies since the Middle Ages. The term "cottage pie" was apparently coined in the late 1700s in Scotland and northern England, referring to a pie made of leftover beef or mutton scraps baked with a top crust of mashed potatoes. The term "shepherd's pie," however, did not appear until the 1870s, with the invention of a meat-mincing machine. According to Wikipedia.org, "There is now a popular tendency for 'shepherd's pie' to be used when the meat is mutton or lamb, with the suggested origin being that shepherds are concerned with sheep and not cattle." The following is a very common and soul-warming modern version of shepherd's pie, using ground beef.

Top Layer

4 large potatoes, peeled and cut into
    large chunks
1 tablespoon butter
1 tablespoon milk
1 tablespoon finely chopped onion
½ cup grated cheddar cheese
salt and pepper, to taste

Meat and Vegetable Layer

1 pound ground beef
1 teaspoon salt
1 tablespoon vegetable oil
½ onion, finely chopped
2 carrots, sliced
1 to 2 celery ribs, sliced
½ cup peas
½ cup corn
2 tablespoons flour
1 tablespoon ketchup
¾ cup beef broth

In a large pot of salted water, boil the potato chunks until they are tender. Drain the potatoes, then mash them with the butter, milk, 1 tablespoon onion, and ¼ cup cheddar cheese. Set aside.

Preheat oven to 375°F. In a large skillet, brown the beef in the oil with the salt, onions, carrots, and celery. Stir in the peas, corn, flour, ketchup, and broth. Bring to a boil, then reduce heat and simmer for about 5 minutes.

Spread the beef mixture in a 2-quart casserole dish, then spread the mashed potatoes evenly over the beef. Sprinkle ¼ cup cheese over the top. Bake for 20 to 25 minutes or until golden brown.

☞ *A cow with its tail to the east makes weather the least.*

→DUTCH OVEN BEEF AND NOODLE CASSEROLE←

This recipe originated in Ireland and is very much like a ground-beef stew.

> 1 pound ground beef
> ½ cup chopped onion
> 2 cups corn
> ⅔ cup sliced mushrooms
> 1 bell pepper, chopped
> 1 teaspoon salt (or to taste)
> ¼ teaspoon pepper
> ½ cup beef broth
> 10 to 12 ounces egg noodles
> 2 cups grated cheddar cheese
> 2 large tomatoes, diced

Heat a Dutch oven to medium high-heat, then brown the beef with the onions, salt, and pepper. Stir in the corn, mushrooms, bell pepper, and broth.

Spread the uncooked noodles on top, then sprinkle the cheese over the noodles. Spread the tomatoes (with the juice) over the top.

Cover the Dutch oven tightly, reduce heat to medium-low, and cook for 1 hour. Turn off the heat, remove the lid, and let the casserole sit for at least 5 minutes before serving.

→MACHACA←

Machaca was developed by ranchers and cowboys from Northern Mexico, particularly the state of Chihuahua. By marinating and pounding the meat (mostly beef) and then dehydrating it, they were able to have meat on the trail. It was commonly served on tortillas and/or with eggs. This version of machaca is not dehydrated, so it is similar to the reconstituted version.

Marinade

> ¼ cup Worcestershire sauce
> juice of 2 limes
> 1 teaspoon garlic powder
> 1 teaspoon ground cumin
> 1 teaspoon chili powder
> ½ teaspoon salt
> ½ teaspoon pepper
> ½ cup vegetable oil

Machaca

2- to 3-pound chuck roast, cut into 3
   or 4 large pieces
1 large yellow onion, diced
½ bell pepper, diced
4 garlic cloves, minced
1 jalapeno, minced (for a very spicy
   flavor, include the seeds)
1 large tomato, diced
½ cup beef broth
1 tablespoon dried oregano
1 tablespoon ground cumin
1 teaspoon Tabasco sauce
salt and pepper, to taste
3 tablespoons vegetable oil

Make the marinade, whisking the ingredients together. Place the meat in a bowl and pour the marinade over it, making sure all of the meat is covered. Cover the bowl with plastic wrap and refrigerate overnight. Then remove the bowl from the fridge, drain the marinade, and set the bowl on the counter for about 30 minutes to allow the meat to come to room temperature.

In a large soup pot over medium heat, sear the beef pieces in the vegetable oil. Turn the pieces so that all sides are brown. Then remove the beef from the pan and sauté the onions, bell pepper, garlic, and jalapeno for 2 to 3 minutes. Return the beef to the pot and add the remaining ingredients. Bring to a boil, then cover and simmer for about 2 hours. The meat is done when you can easily pull it apart with a fork.

☞ *Farmer at the plough,*
Wife milking cow,
Daughter spinning yarn,
Son threshing in the barn,
All happy to a charm.

→MOULDASH←

This noodle dish was brought to America by German immigrants. When German pioneers cooked, it was not uncommon to find them using eggshells as measuring tools.

Broth

> 8 cups water
> 6 beef bouillon cubes

Filling

> ½ pound ground beef
> ½ pound pork sausage
> 1 cup breadcrumbs
> 2 eggs
> ½ teaspoon salt
> ½ teaspoon parsley flakes
> ¼ teaspoon pepper

Noodles

> 2 eggs, beaten
> ⅓ cup milk
> ½ teaspoon salt

> ½ teaspoon baking powder
> 1 to 1¼ cups flour

In a large pot over medium heat, stir the water and bouillon cubes together. In a mixing bowl, thoroughly combine the filling ingredients, then set aside.

Place the noodle ingredients in a separate mixing bowl and knead them together. On a floured surface, roll out the dough, then cut into 2-inch squares.

Put about a teaspoon of filling in the center of each square. Fold each noodle in half, then join the sides with a fork. Gently place each stuffed noodle in the cooking broth and cook for 25 to 30 minutes or until the meat inside is fully cooked.

☞ *When you get old and cannot see, put your specks on and look at me.*

⇾CHICKEN POT PIE⇽

Originally, pot pies were meat and vegetable mixtures that were lined with pie crust and cooked in deep pots. This was done to protect the food from the flavor of the metal pot; the crust was not eaten.

Crust

2 cups flour
1 cup shortening
1 teaspoon salt
½ cup cold water

Filling

1 pound boneless chicken, cut into chunks
1 carrot, sliced
1 celery stalk, sliced
1 medium potato, diced
½ cup peas (frozen are fine)
¼ cup chopped onion
⅓ cup butter
⅓ cup flour
½ teaspoon salt
¼ teaspoon pepper
¼ teaspoon celery seed
1½ cups chicken broth
¾ cup milk

Preheat oven to 425ºF. In a large mixing bowl, cream together the flour, shortening, and salt, then stir in the cold water. Roll out the dough into 2 large circles. Line a 10-inch pie plate with one of the dough circles.

In a large skillet, combine all of the filling ingredients and boil for 10 to 15 minutes.

Scoop the chicken and vegetables into the bottom pie crust, then pour the liquid over the mixture, leaving a little space at the top.

Place the second crust on top, then seal the edges with wet fingers. Cut off excess crust and flute the edges. Cut 3 to 6 small slits in the top crust for ventilation.

Bake for 30 to 35 minutes or until the filling is bubbly and the crust is golden brown. Allow pie to cool for at least 10 minutes before serving.

☞ *Procrastination is the thief of time.*

→CORNISH PASTIES (MEAT PIES)←

The original pasties were predominantly eaten by British miners, farmers, and fishermen. These laborers would hold the pie by the crust, eat the insides, and throw the edges away because it would be dirty from their hands. The Cornish pasty was brought to the United States by British immigrants, and it was a common favorite among pioneers.

Crust

- 2 cups flour
- 1 cup shortening
- 1 teaspoon salt
- ½ cup cold water

In a large mixing bowl, cream together the flour, shortening, and salt. Stir in the cold water. Roll out the dough into 5- to 6-inch circles.

Filling

- ½ pound meat (chicken, pork, or beef), cut into chunks
- 3 potatoes, cut into small chunks
- 3 carrots, sliced
- 1 onion, chopped
- salt and pepper, to taste

Preheat oven to 375ºF. In a mixing bowl, stir together the filling ingredients.

Place about ½ cup of filling on one side of each dough circle. Fold the dough over to cover the filling, then bind the edges (if the dough is too dry, you may need to use wet fingertips). Crimp the edges with a fork.

Cut 2 or 3 slits in the top of each pie for ventilation, then bake for 45 to 50 minutes or until the meat is thoroughly cooked.

☞ *Hope is a good breakfast but a bad supper.*

⟩FRIED CHICKEN⟨

Scottish immigrants brought the concept of fried chicken to the United States; other European immigrants usually baked or boiled their chicken. Many Scots settled in the Southern states, and the wealthier ones had African slaves. Unable to raise beef and other expensive animals, slaves often raised chickens and prepared fried chicken to celebrate special occasions. In plantation kitchens, slaves who worked as cooks would add spices and seasonings not found in the traditional Scottish fried chicken, and American fried chicken was born.

2 to 3 pounds chicken pieces
3 eggs
⅓ cup water
½ teaspoon salt
½ teaspoon onion powder
½ teaspoon garlic salt
¼ teaspoon cayenne pepper
2 cups flour
1 teaspoon pepper
oil for frying

Fill a deep pot about half full with cooking oil. Heat the oil to about 350°F.

In a small mixing bowl, whisk together the eggs and water. In another small mixing bowl, stir together the salt, onion powder, garlic salt, and cayenne pepper. On a dinner plate, stir together the flour and pepper.

Lay out the chicken pieces and sprinkle them with the seasoning mixture, lightly dusting all sides. Drag each piece of chicken in the egg mixture, then the flour mixture, fully coating all sides of each piece with flour.

Carefully lower the chicken pieces into the hot oil and deep fry for 8 to 13 minutes, depending on the size and color of the pieces (dark meat takes a little longer to cook than light meat).

☞ *If you would have a hen lay, you must bear with her cackling.*

→DUTCH OVEN CHICKEN←

Chicken dinners were rare on the trail, since there was no refrigeration and since live chickens do not travel well. But once the pioneers established settlements in the West, most families raised chickens to provide both eggs and meat.

> 5 chicken breasts, skinned
> 1 onion, sliced
> 1 green bell pepper, sliced
> 1½ cups buttermilk
> 1½ cups sour cream
> 6 ounces mushrooms
> 3 large potatoes, peeled and thinly
>   sliced
> 4 large carrots, peeled and sliced
> 2 garlic cloves, minced
> 1½ teaspoons salt
> 2 tablespoons olive oil

In a Dutch oven over medium heat, sauté the onions, garlic, mushrooms, and pepper in the oil for about 3 minutes.

Stir in the potatoes and carrots; sauté for about 4 minutes.

Stir in the remaining ingredients, then cover and reduce heat to medium low. Cook for 1½ hours, stirring every 15 to 20 minutes. The dish is done when the vegetables are tender and the chicken is cooked throughout and tender.

→CHICKEN FRIED STEAK←

Wiener schnitzel, *a dish made with veal or a tenderized beef cutlet, was brought to Texas in the 19th century by German and Austrian immigrants. Around the 1930s, people began calling it "chicken fried steak," probably due to the war with Germany and because the dish is prepared much like fried chicken (see http://en.wikipedia.org/wiki/Chicken_fried_steak). Chicken fried steak is always served with white, peppered, creamy milk gravy (recipe follows).*

> 4 steaks, well tenderized with a meat
>   mallet (or have your butcher
>   run the steaks through a cubing
>   machine)
> 1 cup flour
> ½ teaspoon cracked pepper, divided
> 1 teaspoon salt

½ teaspoon garlic salt
1 cup buttermilk
oil for frying

Heat about ½ cup of oil in a heavy skillet over medium heat. On a plate, stir together the flour and ¼ teaspoon cracked pepper.

In a small bowl, stir together the salt, garlic salt, and remaining ¼ teaspoon cracked pepper. Pour the buttermilk in a bowl wide enough for the steaks to be dipped in.

Sprinkle the salt mixture over both sides of each steak. Drag the seasoned steaks through the buttermilk on both sides, then through the flour mixture, coating both sides completely and evenly.

Fry the steaks in the hot oil, in batches if necessary, for about 6 minutes on each side, or until the crust is dark golden brown and the meat is well done in the center.

☞ *Expect rain if a cow kicks backwards in the morning while she's being milked.*

＊MILK GRAVY＊

This gravy is a very old and simple recipe. Milk gravy is still popular in the southern United States and is typically served with chicken fried steak and biscuits.

    1 cup milk
    2 tablespoons meat drippings
      (optional)
    2 tablespoons flour
    ½ teaspoon salt
    ¼ to ⅓ teaspoon cracked pepper

Heat all ingredients in a saucepan, whisking while cooking. Bring to a boil, then simmer for about 5 minutes before serving.

☞ *If wisdom's ways you'd wisely keep,
Five things observe with care:
Of whom you speak, to whom you speak,
And how, and when, and where.*

⤏BOUDIN⤎

Boudin is a Cajun sausage typically made from pork, chicken, and/or alligator meat. Created by French settlers in Louisiana, the sausage dates back to the early 1800s. When the Lewis and Clark expedition arrived at the Upper Missouri villages in October 1804, a French-Canadian fur trader named Toussaint Charbonneau served the explorers a batch of boudin made from buffalo meat and kidneys (see http://www.pbs.org/lewisandclark/inside/tchar.html).

3½ pounds chicken, pork, or
    alligator meat (with the fat
    trimmed off)
2 quarts water
1 cup chopped onion
2 garlic cloves, minced
½ cup chopped bell pepper
½ cup chopped celery
1½ tablespoons salt
1 tablespoon cayenne pepper
1½ teaspoons black pepper
1 cup chopped parsley
1 cup chopped green onions
6 cups steamed rice
1½-inch-diameter sausage casings
    (about 4 feet long)

In a large pot, combine the meat, water, onion, garlic, bell pepper, celery, 1 teaspoon salt, ¼ teaspoon cayenne pepper, and ¼ teaspoon black pepper. Bring the mixture to a boil, then simmer for about 2 hours, or until the meat is very tender.

Remove the meat from the pot, reserving 1½ cups of broth. Grind the pork mixture in a meat grinder along with ½ cup parsley and ½ cup green onions.

In a large mixing bowl, combine the ground pork with the steamed rice and the remaining parsley, green onions, salt, cayenne pepper, and black pepper. Stir in the 1½ cups of reserved broth half a cup at a time, stirring well after each addition.

Using a funnel, stuff the casings with the sausage, making 4-inch links. In a large pot of water, boil the sausages for about 5 minutes or until they become firm.

→SAUSAGE GRAVY←

Sausage gravy was originally called "sawmill gravy" and is still known by that name in many Southern states. The term "sawmill" came from cornmeal, which gave the gravy a gritty texture, though it probably doesn't taste much like sawdust. Sausage gravy is traditionally served over fresh-baked buttermilk biscuits (see page 118).

> 1 pound ground pork sausage
> 1 tablespoon flour
> 1 tablespoon cornmeal
> ½ teaspoon salt
> ½ teaspoon onion powder
> ¼ teaspoon cracked pepper
> 1½ cups milk

Crumble the sausage and brown it in a heavy skillet. Remove the sausage and drain all of the grease from the pan except 2 tablespoons.

Whisk the remaining grease with the flour, cornmeal, salt, onion powder, pepper, and milk. Bring to a boil, stirring frequently, then return the sausage to the gravy. Simmer for a few more minutes before serving.

→FRIED SALT PORK←

As the name implies, salt pork is pork that has been cured with salt. It resembles uncut slab bacon but is not smoked and is considerably saltier than bacon. It is one of the few meats, in addition to dried jerky, that travels well without refrigeration. Therefore, it was a staple food among pioneers.

> 1 pound fat salt pork, thinly sliced

In a heavy skillet, fry the sliced pork, turning frequently until well browned.

Crisp salt pork is often served as an accompaniment to creamed dried beef over baked potatoes. It may also be served with a cream gravy. To make the gravy, add 1 cup thick cream to 1 tablespoon of the salt-pork fat left in the pan. As soon as the cream is hot, pour it over the cooked salt-pork slices.

☞ *May your friends be many, your troubles few, and all your sausages long.*

→DUTCH OVEN PORK CHOPS AND VEGETABLES←

Pork chops, referred to simply as "chops" by most pioneers, were typically a breakfast food.

  six 1-inch-thick pork chops
  3 tablespoons butter
  3 carrots, sliced ½ inch thick
  ½ onion, sliced
  1 teaspoon salt
  1 teaspoon garlic salt
  ¼ teaspoon pepper
  1½ cups fresh green beans, cut into
     1-inch pieces
  2 large potatoes, peeled and cut into
     chunks

Heat the Dutch oven on the stove over medium heat. Melt the butter and brown the pork chops on both sides.

Remove the chops, drain the butter and grease, and place the vegetables on the bottom of the Dutch oven. Place the pork chops on the vegetables. Add the seasonings and cover with water.

Bring to a boil, then cover and reduce heat to medium low. Cook for about 45 minutes or until the pork chops and vegetables are tender.

→SHEPHERD'S PIE←

This version of shepherd's pie was commonly eaten by sheepherders settling the western part of the United States (particularly Idaho), who needed to make simple, filling meals over a fire. Shepherd's pie is known as a "poor man's meal," and this version is made with bacon rather than minced lamb or beef.

  5 slices bacon
  2 large potatoes, peeled and thinly
     sliced
  1 green onion, sliced
  1 tablespoon parsley flakes
  ½ teaspoon salt
  ¼ teaspoon thyme flakes
  ¼ teaspoon pepper

3 eggs

2 tablespoons milk

Cook the bacon in a skillet until crisp. Crumble the bacon and drain all but about 2 tablespoons of drippings.

Return the bacon to the skillet and stir in the potatoes, onion, and seasonings. Cover and cook over medium heat for 10 to 12 minutes, or until the potatoes are tender.

In a separate bowl, beat the milk and eggs together. Pour the egg mixture over the potatoes, then cover the skillet and let cook until the eggs are no longer runny.

⇢HONEY HAM⇠

Early settlers of Jamestown brought pigs from England and Scotland and continued the centuries-long tradition of slaughtering the animals in mid-November. Today, ham— along with turkey— is still a staple for many Thanksgiving and Christmas celebrations.

6- to 7-pound fully cooked bone-in
   ham

½ cup brown sugar

½ cup honey

¼ cup molasses

¼ cup butter

Preheat oven to 375°F. Cut a diamond pattern of slits in the ham about ¼ to ½ inch deep. Place the ham in a large roasting pan.

In a small saucepan, heat and stir the remaining ingredients until a syrup is formed. Generously spread the syrup on all sides of the ham.

Place a foil tent over the ham, avoiding direct contact between the foil and the ham. Bake ham for about 1 hour, basting every 20 minutes with the syrup and the pan drippings.

Remove the foil tent, then broil the ham for about 10 minutes or until it has turned a nice brown color.

☞ *If you hold lizard eggs in your hands, you'll break plates.*

⁕TRAILBLAZER BEANS⁕

Beans were a staple among frontiers people due to the legumes' hearty and nourishing qualities. Beans could be stored dry for long periods of time, making them invaluable on the trail.

> 1 pound dried pinto beans
> 8 cups water
> 1 pound ham hocks
> ½ cup chopped onion
> ½ cup diced tomatoes
> 2 tablespoons sugar
> 1 teaspoon salt (or to taste)

Soak beans overnight if possible, then drain and cook in a large stockpot with remaining ingredients for about an hour and a half.

Remove ham hocks, pull the bone away from the meat, and return the meat to the beans. Discard the bones. If you have not soaked the beans, simply cook them for an additional 1½ hours or until they are tender.

☞ *The bread never falls but on its buttered side.*

⁕HOMEMADE SAUSAGE⁕

You'll need a meat grinder to make sausage. The word sausage *is derived from the Latin* salsus, *which means "salt." Centuries ago, when refrigeration was not available in the warmer climates of Europe, people would pack meat in salt as a method of preservation. Sausage was originally considered a poor man's meat and was made from lesser cuts of meat and from meat scraps.*

> 1 pound lean pork
> 1 teaspoons fennel seeds
> ⅔ teaspoon salt
> ½ teaspoon sage
> ½ teaspoon pepper

Grind the pork with a meat grinder. Then, using your hands and a large mixing bowl, mix the ground pork and spices together well.

Most recipes call for loose rather than encased sausage, but if you choose to put the sausage in casings, get them fresh from the butcher. Before using the casings, rinse them in cold water and let them soak for 30 minutes. After stuffing the sausage into the casings, twist the ends.

☞ *Green eye, greedy gut,*
Steal a pig and eat it up;
Brown eye, picket pie;
Run around and tell a lie!

→RED BEANS AND RICE←

Red beans and rice is a native Caribbean dish that was brought to America by slaves. This dish became popular in the French Quarter of New Orleans and was spread abroad as Cajun cuisine. It was traditionally served on Mondays because the ham bone in it was left over from Sunday dinner, and because Monday was wash day and this meal could cook slowly all day, needing little attention, while the women scrubbed clothes.

1 pound dried kidney beans
8 cups water
ham bone (optional)
1 onion, diced
2 celery stalks, sliced
1 green or red chili pepper (stem and
 seeds removed), diced
2 cloves garlic, minced
1½ teaspoons salt (or to taste)
1½ cups dried rice

Rinse the beans, then place all ingredients except the rice in a large stockpot. Cover and cook on medium heat for 3 to 4 hours, stirring occasionally.

Stir the rice into the pot for the last 30 minutes of cooking. It may be necessary to add more water if it cooks out before the rice is soft.

The beans and rice are done when they are tender. Remove the ham bone before serving.

☞ *Speech is silver, but silence*
is golden.

⇀JAMBALAYA↽

Jambalaya is a traditional Cajun dish that was developed from French and Spanish influences in the French Quarter of New Orleans. The dish usually contains seafood, sausage, and/or chicken, but it may be made with crawdads, alligator, duck, or turtle.

1 dozen shrimp, deveined* and
   chopped
2 cups ground sausage
2 tablespoons olive oil
¼ cup chopped onion
¼ cup chopped bell pepper
¼ cup chopped celery
2 garlic cloves, minced
½ cup chopped tomatoes
2 bay leaves
1 tablespoon Worcestershire sauce
1 to 2 teaspoons Tabasco sauce
¾ cup rice
3 cups broth (any kind)
1 teaspoon salt
1 teaspoon paprika
½ teaspoon garlic powder
½ teaspoon onion powder
½ teaspoon oregano
½ teaspoon thyme
½ teaspoon cayenne pepper
¼ teaspoon black pepper

In a large saucepan over medium heat, sauté the shrimp and sausage until the sausage is just browned (3 to 5 minutes), stirring frequently.

Stir in the remaining ingredients. Cover the pan and let cook until the liquid is absorbed and the rice is done. (If the rice isn't done when the liquid is gone, add a little more water, then cover the pan and cook a little longer.) Stir occasionally while cooking.

*To devein shrimp, cut a slit along the outer curve of each shrimp, where a dark vein can be seen through the skin. Remove the vein and any noticeable debris. Rinse deveined shrimp with cold water.

⇀CRAB CAKES↽

Crab cakes have been popular since colonial times. They were brought to America by English immigrants.

1 pound crab meat

⅓ cup breadcrumbs

3 green onions, finely chopped

½ cup diced green bell pepper

¼ cup mayonnaise

1 egg

1 teaspoon Worcestershire sauce

1 teaspoon prepared mustard

juice of ½ lemon

¼ teaspoon garlic powder

1 teaspoon salt

dash of cayenne pepper

flour for dusting

½ cup vegetable oil

Heat the oil in a large skillet over medium heat. In a large mixing bowl, combine all remaining ingredients except the flour. Form the crab mixture into 3-inch cakes, then lightly dust the cakes with flour.

Place the cakes in the hot oil in batches. Cook crab cakes for 3 to 4 minutes or until the bottoms turn golden brown. Carefully flip cakes over and cook for another 3 to 4 minutes. Remove cakes from oil and place on paper towels to dry. Serve warm with cocktail or tartar sauce.

→BOILED LOBSTER←

The ancient Romans and Greeks enjoyed eating boiled lobster. The dish was also highly favored by the British. However, Americans didn't really care for it until the 19th century.

2 live lobsters

1 lemon

2 tablespoons butter

Fill a large stockpot ¾ full with salted water. Bring the water to a rolling boil. Place the lobsters upside down in the pot, then cover with a lid. Allow the water to return to a boil and continue to boil another 15 to 20 minutes. Place the lobsters in a large bowl or plate to drain.

In a separate saucepan melt the butter with the juice from the lemon (pulp included).

Serve the lemon–butter sauce with the lobster, letting diners break and pick apart the lobster themselves.

☞ *Self-praise is no recommendation.*

⁺FRIED SHRIMP⁺

Before the invention of the ice machine in the early 1900s, shrimp were eaten exclusively in the cities and islands along the Gulf of Mexico. To catch shrimp, shrimpers used flat-bottom boats called luggers because they could easily navigate in shallow bayous and bays. Once they obtained ice machines to preserve their catch, shrimpers began using large shrimp boats and catching farther out at sea.

> 1½ pounds shrimp, deveined (see instructions on page 34) and boiled
> 1 egg
> 2 cups milk
> ¾ cup flour
> ⅓ cup cornmeal
> ⅓ cup fine breadcrumbs
> ¼ teaspoon salt
> ⅛ teaspoon pepper
> oil for frying

Fill a large skillet about halfway with cooking oil. With the burner on medium high, heat the oil to about 370°F.

In a mixing bowl, beat the egg and milk together. Stir the shrimp into the milk mixture and let sit for about 3 minutes.

In a separate bowl, stir together the flour, cornmeal, breadcrumbs, salt, and pepper. Drag the soaked shrimp back and forth in the flour mixture until each shrimp is well coated.

Carefully place the battered shrimp in the hot oil and cook until golden brown and crispy (about 4 to 6 minutes). Drain on paper towels and serve with cocktail sauce and/or tartar sauce.

☞ *The fish sees the bait but not the hook.*
CHINESE PROVERB

Preparing the Catch of the Day

When possible, pioneers stayed close to water. They were quite inventive when it came to finding water in desperate situations, but the majority of trails and settlements were purposely situated near rivers, streams, and/or lakes. When a frontiersman caught a fish, he knew just what to do with it.

All fish are tender and should be baked, poached, fried, or broiled. The most common and simple seasonings for fish on the trail were salt, pepper, and onions.

Step 1: Soak fish in cold water for a few minutes

Step 2: While holding the fish firmly, scrape a dull knife from the tail to the head repeatedly until all of the scales have been removed.

Step 3: Using a sharp knife, cut into the fish's belly from its tail to its gills. Pull out the skeleton and entrails.

Step 4: Cut around and pull out all fins.

Step 5: Cut off the head.

Step 6: Quickly rinse the fish in cold water, then wipe dry.

Step 7: Cook small fish whole. Larger fish can be cut lengthwise into fillets or widthwise into steaks.

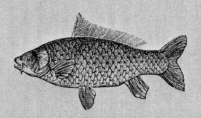

→PAN-FRIED TROUT←

Pioneers enjoyed eating freshly caught wild trout, and frying was the easiest way to cook the fish. Serve with a side of creamy mashed potatoes and steamed Swiss chard.

> 1 pound (1 or 2 whole) trout,
>   cleaned (see "Preparing the Catch
>   of the Day," page 37)
> 2 tablespoons butter
> ¾ cup all-purpose flour
> salt and pepper

Clean fish. Be sure to remove gills even if you leave fish heads on.

Season flour with salt and pepper, then spread flour on a dinner plate. Dredge fish in flour to coat thoroughly. Cook fish in butter in a skillet, turning over once, until the flesh flakes with a fork.

→BAKED TROUT←

In the early 1800s, a 12-inch brook trout could be bought at market for 25 cents, a small fortune in those days. As Cervantes declared, "There's no taking trout with dry breeches."

> 1 trout, cleaned (see "Preparing the
>   Catch of the Day," page 37)
> juice from 1 lemon
> 1 tablespoon chopped lemon rind
> salt and pepper, to taste

Preheat oven to 350ºF. Rub lemon juice all over the trout, then place on an oiled baking pan. Sprinkle with the lemon rind and generous amounts of salt and pepper.

Bake for 20 to 30 minutes or until the flesh flakes easily with a fork.

Drizzle some (or all) of the remaining lemon juice on the fish before serving.

☞ *A fat kitchen, a lean will.*

→FRIED CATFISH←

Southerners love to fry just about anything, and catfish is no exception, especially among residents along the Gulf of Mexico, where catfish breed in abundance in the bayous, ponds, and lakes of the region. In fact, hosting a party where catfish are fried and eaten—a "catfish fry"—is an old tradition among Southerners.

⅓ cup buttermilk
⅓ cup milk
⅓ cup water
salt and pepper, to taste
1 to 1½ pounds catfish fillets (cut into strips to make fish sticks, if desired)
1½ cups cornmeal
1 teaspoon lemon pepper
oil for frying

Pour oil into a skillet until it is about ¾ inch deep. With burner on medium high, heat the oil to about 360°F.

Spread the catfish fillets on a plate and season with salt and pepper. In a mixing bowl, whisk together the buttermilk, milk, and water. In a large bowl, combine the fillets with the milk mixture, gently stirring to fully coat each side.

Combine the cornmeal and lemon pepper in a gallon ziptop plastic bag. Carefully place the fillets in the bag with the cornmeal mix, then seal the bag. Gently turn the bag back and forth, slightly shaking it, to fully coat each side of each fillet.

Carefully place the battered fish into the hot oil in batches. Fry for about 3 minutes on each side, or until golden brown and crispy. Drain fish on paper towels.

☞ *Ask no questions and hear no lies.*

⇸STUFFED FLOUNDER⇷

There is a substantial population of flounder off the Atlantic Coast, towards the more northern colonies. Early immigrant fishermen would catch flounder for dinner and to sell at market.

2 pounds flounder fillets
½ cup chopped onion
½ teaspoon salt plus salt and pepper, to taste
1 garlic clove, minced
1 cup chopped spinach, firmly packed
2 tablespoons lemon juice
2 tablespoons chopped parsley
1 cup heavy cream
¼ cup butter, melted
2 cups grated cheddar cheese
3 cups steamed wild rice

Split the thick side of the flounders lengthwise and widthwise. Loosen the flesh from the bones and separate the sides to form a pocket. Generously brush the lemon juice and 2 tablespoons of the butter inside the pocket, then salt and pepper all sides of the fish. Set aside.

In a saucepan, sauté the onion, garlic, spinach, and parsley in the remaining butter for about 5 minutes over medium heat. In a large mixing bowl, mix the sautéed vegetables with the cream, grated cheese, steamed wild rice, and ½ teaspoon salt.

Fill the flounder pockets with the stuffing. Place the fish in a baking dish, then add enough water to cover the bottom of the dish. Lightly cover the dish with foil and bake for about 30 minutes at 350°F, basting the top of the fish often with the pan juices.

⇸POTATO CROQUETTES⇷

According to an Irish legend, in the late 1500s, a Spanish armada wrecked near the coast and some potatoes washed onto shore, and that is how potatoes came to Ireland. Many American pioneers from Europe lived off the potato quite heavily, none so much as the settlers of Idaho.

1 cup milk
2 tablespoons butter, melted
2 tablespoons flour

2 large potatoes, finely chopped or
    grated
1 egg yolk
1 teaspoon salt
¼ teaspoon onion salt
¼ teaspoon pepper
bowl of breadcrumbs
1 egg, well beaten
lard or vegetable oil for frying

Cover the bottom surface of a large frying pan with lard or vegetable oil. Place on the stove at medium heat.

In a large mixing bowl, whisk together the milk, butter, and flour. Add the potatoes, egg yolk, salt, onion salt, and pepper; mix thoroughly.

Form the dough into small balls. Roll the potato balls in the breadcrumbs, then in the beaten egg, then in the breadcrumbs again. Carefully place the potato balls in the hot oil and cook for about 5 minutes, watching closely and stirring often to cook on all sides.

☞ *A rotten apple spoils*
its companion.

⇢POTATO HASH⇠

Though potato hash was occasionally served as a main dish, it was usually served with beef, particularly corned beef (see page 18), and often with eggs.

1 large potato, diced
2 tablespoons vegetable broth
½ cup chopped onion
½ cup chopped green bell pepper
½ cup chopped red bell pepper
¾ cup corn
1 teaspoon salt
½ teaspoon pepper
2 tablespoons butter

Boil the potatoes in water until tender, then drain. Combine the broth, peppers, onion, and corn in a skillet and sauté for 5 to 10 minutes over medium heat.

Add the vegetables to the potatoes, then season with salt and pepper. Melt the butter in the skillet and add the potato–vegetable mixture. Stir occasionally and continue cooking until the potatoes start to turn golden brown.

→HASH BROWN CASSEROLE←

Hash browns used to be called "hashed browned potatoes." The name evolved to "hash brown potatoes," then eventually to simply "hash browns" in the 1970s.

2 large potatoes, peeled and grated
2 cups grated cheddar cheese
¼ cup finely chopped onion
1 cup milk
½ cup vegetable broth
2 tablespoons butter, melted
1 teaspoon salt
¼ teaspoon pepper
⅛ teaspoon garlic powder

Preheat oven to 425°F. Lightly coat an 8-inch square baking dish with butter.

In a large bowl, combine the potatoes, cheese, and onion.

In a separate bowl, stir together the remaining ingredients.

Spread the potato mixture into the prepared baking dish, then pour the liquid mixture over the potatoes.

Bake for 1 hour, stirring after 30 minutes.

→LUMPY DICK←

Lumpy dick originated in Scandinavia. "Dick" means some type of pudding.

4 cups scalding-hot milk
1½ cups flour
2 eggs
1 teaspoon salt
1 tablespoon sugar
1 teaspoon vanilla
dash of nutmeg

While the milk is heating, beat together the flour, eggs, and salt in a separate bowl (the mixture will be very lumpy).

Stir the mixture into the scalding milk (it will be very thick). Remove the pan from the heat, then stir in the sugar, vanilla, and nutmeg.

→MILK TOAST←

Milk toast was very popular in the 19th century, especially among young children and people who were ailing. It was considered a comfort food.

2 pieces of toasted bread
½ cup warm milk
2 teaspoons sugar

Stir the sugar into the warm milk until it is dissolved. Then dip the toast into the milk, mopping it up with the toast. May also be served with nutmeg, vanilla, and/or raisins.

→POACHED EGGS←

In the late 1800s, poached eggs gained popularity among the Eastern states, then rapidly spread throughout the rest of the nation with the invention of eggs Benedict.

6 cups boiling water
1 tablespoon white vinegar
desired number of eggs (cook one at a time)

Have the eggs, one at a time, cracked and ready in a small bowl.

Boil the water with the vinegar, then remove pan from heat. Using a large wooden spoon, stir the hot water around to create a whirlpool effect. While continuing to stir, gently pour the cracked egg into the center of the whirlpool, touching the egg with the back of the spoon.

Return the pan to heat and allow the egg to boil until the white is cooked and the yolk is still runny.

☞ *Nothing helps scenery like ham and eggs.*

⭢DANISH OMELET⭠

The omelet probably originated in the ancient Near East. According to wikipedia.org, "Beaten eggs were mixed with chopped herbs, fried until firm, then sliced into wedges. This dish is thought to have traveled to Western Europe via the Middle East and North Africa, with each country adapting the original recipe to produce Italian frittata, Spanish tortilla, and the French omelette." The following is a traditional Danish farmer's dish.

    8 large eggs
    ⅓ cup milk
    2 teaspoons flour
    salt and pepper, to taste

Toppings

    6 medium-thick slices of bacon
    1 tomato, sliced thinly
    chives, chopped

Beat the eggs well in a medium bowl. Combine flour and milk in a cup and then add to beaten eggs, stirring well. Add salt and pepper as desired.

Fry the bacon in a large, dry skillet. Remove bacon from skillet and add eggs to skillet. Lower heat to medium and cook the eggs in the bacon grease until they reach the desired consistency.

Place bacon, tomato slices, and chopped chives on top of omelet. Serve hot with rye bread and butter.

⭢EGGS BENEDICT⭠

Eggs Benedict was invented in the late 1800s by Mrs. Le Grand Benedict, who ate regularly at Delmonico's in New York. Apparently, she became tired of the restaurant's menu and asked the kitchen to whip her up this tasty meal. The idea spread rapidly across the nation as a popular breakfast entrée.

    2 English muffins, sliced in half
    4 slices Canadian bacon
    4 to 8 poached eggs
    hollandaise sauce (see page 45)

Toast the English muffin slices. Grill the Canadian bacon, or sear it in a hot frying pan. Place the Canadian bacon slices on the toasted English muffin halves, then the poached eggs atop the Canadian bacon. Drizzle hollandaise sauce over the eggs.

→HOLLANDAISE SAUCE←

4 egg yolks
3½ tablespoons lemon juice
pinch of pepper
⅛ teaspoon Worcestershire sauce
1 tablespoon water
1 cup butter, melted
¼ teaspoon salt
¼ teaspoon lemon zest (optional)

Fill the bottom of a double boiler halfway and bring the water to a simmer. In the top of the double boiler, whisk together the yolks, lemon juice, pepper, Worcestershire sauce, and water.

Slowly whisk in the melted butter, then the salt and lemon zest. Remove sauce from heat and keep covered until ready to use.

☞ *Betty Botter bought some butter.*
"But," she said, "this butter's bitter.
If I put this bitter butter in my batter,
It would make my batter bitter.
But a bit of better butter
Would but make my bitter batter better."
So Betty Botter bought some butter,
Better than the bitter butter.
Made her bitter batter better.

☞ *Never serve turkey on New Year's or you will scratch backwards. Always serve pork to root forward.*

→POBLANO ENCHILADAS←

Among the Aztec people of Mexico, enchiladas were a common dish in the 1800s, though the first enchiladas—small fish wrapped in tortillas—probably originated hundreds of years earlier. Tex-Mex-style enchiladas are traditionally served with a creamy sauce like sour cream and pico de gallo, along with rice and beans.

1 poblano pepper, stem and seeds removed

1 chili pepper, stem and seeds removed

2 garlic cloves

1½ cups fresh spinach, firmly packed

1½ cups shredded Monterrey Jack or cheddar cheese

12 tortillas

1 large tomato

1 red bell pepper, stem and seeds removed

½ onion

¼ cup cilantro

2 teaspoons salt

1 teaspoon lime juice

Preheat oven to 350°F. In a food processer or blender, chop the poblano pepper, chili pepper, 1 garlic clove, and spinach until they are still slightly chunky. Put in a bowl and stir in 1 cup shredded cheese and 1 teaspoon salt. Set the filling aside.

Place the tomato, red bell pepper, onion, 1 garlic clove, and cilantro in the food processor or blender; blend until smooth. Place this mixture in a large saucepan. Stir in 1 teaspoon salt and the lime juice. Heat the sauce over medium-low heat.

Have a 9 x 13-inch baking dish ready. Place 1 tortilla at a time in the warm sauce for 10 to 15 seconds, then flip the tortilla over so that both sides are covered with sauce and are flexible but not soggy. Place the tortilla in one end of the baking dish, then spread ¼ to ⅓ cup of the vegetable–cheese filling down the center of the tortilla. Roll up the sides of the tortilla like a burrito. Repeat the process until all of the tortillas and filling have been used.

Spread the remaining sauce over the enchiladas, then sprinkle ½ cup cheese over the top. Bake for 25 to 30 minutes, or until all of the cheese is completely melted.

→PICO DE GALLO←

Pico de gallo *translates to "rooster's beak" in Spanish. It is a fresh, uncooked salsa made primarily of chopped tomatoes, chopped onions, and jalapeno or Serrano chili peppers. Salsas originated with the Mayan, Aztec, and Incan civilizations. According to buzzle.com, Spaniards were introduced to tomatoes during their conquest of Mexico in about 1521. Aztecs combined tomatoes, chili peppers, and ground squash seeds, eating the sauce with turkey, venison, lobster, and fish. In 1571, Alonso de Molina referred to this combination as "salsa," and the name stuck.*

6 roma tomatoes, diced
½ red onion, diced
½ jalapeno pepper, seeded and
    minced
3 tablespoons chopped fresh cilantro
juice of ½ lime
1 garlic clove, minced
⅛ teaspoon garlic powder
⅛ teaspoon ground cumin
salt and black pepper, to taste

In a medium bowl, stir together the tomatoes, onion, jalapeno pepper, cilantro, lime juice, garlic, garlic powder, cumin, salt, and pepper. Refrigerate pico de gallo at least 3 hours before serving.

→TAMALES←

When the Spanish conquistadors arrived in Mexico, they discovered a tasty dish called tamales. The concept of tamales spread to other Spanish colonies, and today most Latin cultures have their own version of the tamale.

8 ounce package dried corn husks
2 cups masa harina
1½ cups vegetable broth, divided
1 teaspoon baking powder
½ teaspoon salt
⅔ cup shortening

In a large bowl of warm water, soak the corn husks until they are soft and flexible.

In a large mixing bowl, combine the shortening with about 1 tablespoon of broth.

In a separate bowl, stir together the masa harina, baking powder, and salt. Add this mixture to the shortening mixture, mixing thoroughly. Add more broth as necessary to make a spongy dough.

Spread the mixture on an unfolded, wet corn husk until the mixture is ½ inch to ¾ inch thick. Roll up the husk and twist each end. Place in the top of a double boiler or steamer; steam for about 1 hour.

➛OPTIONAL CHEESE FILLING FOR TAMALES←

1 pound queso fresco, panela, or
ranchero cheese, cubed
¾ cup salsa

In a bowl, stir the cheese and salsa together. Follow directions for tamales above, but spread only about ¼ inch of masa dough on each husk. Place about 1½ tablespoons of the cheese mixture on top of the masa dough before rolling it up and twisting the ends.

➛OPTIONAL PORK FILLING FOR TAMALES←

2 pounds pork meat, fat trimmed off
5½ cups water
½ onion, chopped
2 garlic cloves, minced
2 teaspoons salt
2 cups red chili sauce

In a large covered pot, boil the pork in the water with the onion, garlic, and salt until the meat is very tender.

Remove the meat from the pan. Chop the meat using two forks, discarding any pieces of fat. Reserve the broth to use in place of the vegetable broth when making the masa dough for these tamales.

Put the red chili sauce in a large saucepan and stir in the chopped meat. Simmer for about 10 minutes.

Follow all instructions for making tamales except spread only ¼ inch of masa dough on the wet corn husks. Then spread about

1½ tablespoons of pork filling over the masa dough before rolling them up and twisting the ends.

→BAKED TAMALE CASSEROLE←

Tamales in Mexico are as popular as sandwiches in the United States. Like sandwiches, tamales are easily portable and can be made with various fillings. It is rumored that tamales date back to about 5000 BC.

12 to 15 tamales (see recipe on page 47)
1½ cups diced tomatoes
1 onion, chopped
1 bell pepper, chopped
2 garlic cloves, minced
2 teaspoons lime juice
2 teaspoons chili powder
1½ teaspoons salt
¼ teaspoon black pepper
1 cup grated cheddar or Monterrey Jack cheese
1 cup sour cream
1 cup sliced black olives
2 cups shredded lettuce

Preheat oven to 350°F. Make a single layer of tamales in a 9 x 13-inch baking dish, laying them side by side. Set aside.

In a large saucepan, stir together the tomatoes, onion, bell pepper, garlic, lime juice, chili powder, salt, and pepper. Cook over medium heat until all vegetables are soft (about 15 minutes). Stir and mash vegetables occasionally while cooking.

Spread the sauce evenly over the tamales. Sprinkle the grated cheese over the top and bake for 25 to 30 minutes or until all of the cheese is completely melted.

Remove the casserole from the oven. Spread the sour cream evenly on top of the casserole. Sprinkle the olives on the sour cream, then top with the shredded lettuce. Serve immediately.

☞ *You can catch more flies with honey than you can with vinegar.*

Preparing Wild Game

These instructions are basic and can be used for just about any animal, large or small. Most homes are not equipped to handle larger game such as deer, boar, or bear, and in such cases it is a good idea to take them to the local butcher and pay the expert to take care of it.

When a pioneer was able to catch a rabbit, opossum, squirrel, or even a skunk, they would most certainly eat it soon for dinner. There are accounts of these quick and able pioneers catching and eating just about any type of animal, from muskrats to buffalo. The technique is pretty much the same for all wild game, with adjustments for the size of the creature. If possible, wear gloves while attempting this procedure.

Step 1: Cut off the head, tail, and front legs.

Step 2: Cut just through the fur and skin around the joint of each leg.

Step 3: Hang the animal upside down by the hind legs (for very small game, working on a table will do).

Step 4: Cut through the skin in a curved line from hind leg to hind leg, and from foreleg to foreleg through the neck opening.

Step 5: Starting at the top, peel the fur and skin down and off, inside out.

Step 6: Slit the belly open, just through the muscle, then take out and discard the entrails (be careful not to cut into the bile sac).

Step 7: Cut off the fat (fat from wild game tastes bad).

Step 8: For small animals, wrap the carcass in a damp towel or put into a plastic bag, then place in the refrigerator. Young animals should be aged for a day before being cooked and eaten. Older animals should be aged in the refrigerator for about four days to become tender enough to cook and eat.

For large game, after step 7, wipe the carcass inside and out with a small towel that has been dipped in a solution of 1 cup water to 1 tablespoon vinegar.

Pioneers on the frontier and trails lived very simply. The common seasonings used for cooking wild game over an open fire (usually in a cast-iron skillet or Dutch oven, or roasted on a spittle) were salt, pepper, thyme, and sage. Onions and potatoes usually accompanied these feasts. The majority of the wild game caught while traveling on the trails was made into a stew or fried in a pan.

→BAKED RABBIT←

For meat, pioneers ate what they could kill or catch, and that often included rabbit. Serve this tasty dish over rice or with pasta or polenta.

> 2- to 3-pound rabbit, cut in serving
> pieces
> 6 tablespoons butter
> 1½ cups fine breadcrumbs
> 1 teaspoon salt
> pepper, to taste
> chopped parsley

Preheat oven to 350°F. Mix cracker crumbs with seasonings. Melt butter in a shallow dish. Dip rabbit pieces in melted butter, then roll in seasoned breadcrumbs.

Place rabbit pieces in a shallow baking dish. Cover the dish with a lid or aluminum foil. Bake for 1 hour or until rabbit is tender and juices run clear.

⇥ROASTED WILD BOAR⇤

Wild boar, or feral swine, are native to Europe, Asia, and North Africa. They were introduced to the Americas by explorers. For centuries, most American wild boars lived in the Gulf Coast region, but now they can be found from Florida to Colorado.

1 loin roast of boar, fat trimmed off
1½ teaspoons salt
1½ teaspoons ground mustard
½ teaspoon thyme flakes
½ teaspoon ground ginger
1½ cups orange juice
½ cup honey
1 orange, sliced but not peeled

Preheat the oven to 300°F. Place the roast in an appropriate-size baking dish.

In a small bowl, combine the spices with ¾ cup of the orange juice and spread on the roast. Bake for 1 hour.

Whisk together the remaining orange juice and honey, then baste the roast with the mixture. Bake for 1 more hour, basting every 15 minutes with the drippings and juice. Bake another 45 minutes or until a meat thermometer placed deep in the roast reaches 185°F. Garnish with the orange slices.

⇥ROASTED RACCOON⇤

Coonskin caps were popular among frontiersman and trappers. These hardy people would trap raccoons, skin them for their fur to make hats and coats, then eat the meat.

1 raccoon, cleaned and cut into
    chunks (see "Preparing Wild
    Game," page 50)
½ cup flour
1 teaspoon salt
½ teaspoon parsley flakes
¼ teaspoon pepper
¼ cup cooking oil
1 large onion, peeled and sliced
1 bay leaf

Preheat oven to 350°F. Heat the oil in a large cast-iron skillet over medium heat.

In a bowl, stir together the flour, salt, parsley, and pepper. Dip the raccoon chunks in the seasoned flour, covering all sides of the meat.

Gently place the meat in the hot oil and stir while cooking until the meat is browned.

Pour out the excess oil. Add the onions and bay leaf, then cover and bake for 2 hours or until tender.

☞ *Slow as molasses in January running up hill.*

Preparing Game Birds

This includes all of the well-eaten birds such as goose, duck, pheasant, chicken, turkey, and so forth, as well as any other bird hunted for food.

Step 1: Boil a large pot of water and melt 1 cake of paraffin wax in it.

Step 2: Cut the bird's head off (some break the neck first if the bird isn't already dead).

Step 3: Dip the bird into the boiling water.

Step 4: Remove the feathers in handfuls.

Step 5: Singe the fuzz off the bird with fire (such as with a lighter), and pluck out any small feathers with tweezers.

Step 5: Cut the skin from the anus to the breastbone.

Step 6: Reach your hand into the body and pull out the entrails. Discard.

Step 7: Cut the tail off.

Step 8: Place the bird in the refrigerator to age before cooking, one day if young and four days if old.

→BAKED TURKEY←

Wild turkey is native to North America and was commonly hunted and eaten by Native Americans. In the early 16th century, when Spaniards imported the bird to Europe by way of Turkey (the country), the English called the bird "turkey," and the name stuck. According to slate.com, "By 1863, when Lincoln proclaimed Thanksgiving a national holiday, turkeys had taken center stage at Thanksgiving. (Americans had started holding unofficial Thanksgiving dinners in the previous century.) And while the bird had already been associated with Christmas, the turkey also gained iconic status as a yuletide meal around the same time."

15- to 20-pound whole turkey
½ cup (1 stick) butter, at room
   temperature
1½ teaspoons salt
½ teaspoon pepper
5 cups turkey stock
2 tablespoons brown sugar
2 tablespoons honey

Preheat oven to 325°F. Place oven rack in the lowest position.

Remove the turkey neck and giblets. Rinse the turkey and pat dry with paper towels. Place the turkey on a rack in a large roasting pan, breast side up. Rub the butter all over the turkey, then evenly sprinkle on the salt and pepper.

Pour 2 cups of stock into the bottom of the roasting pan. Stir the honey and sugar together; stir into the stock in the pan. Cover the turkey with a foil tent.

Bake turkey for about 4 hours, basting with pan juices every 30 minutes. Add more stock as it evaporates. The turkey is fully cooked when a cooking thermometer inserted into the thigh reaches 180°F.

☞ *Assume a virtue if you have it not, and in time it will become your own.*

✦ROASTED DUCK✦

Duck hunting became quite the sport in the 17th century with the invention of the matchlock shotgun. There was a marked increase in commercial duck hunting in the late 1800s because of the rising number of immigrants and the subsequent increase in demand for poultry.

> 1 duck, cleaned and aged (see
>   "Preparing Game Birds," page 53)
> ½ teaspoon salt
> ½ teaspoon pepper
> ½ teaspoon chopped fresh
>   rosemary leaves
> ½ cup butter, melted
> ½ onion, sliced
> 1 apple, cored and sliced but not
>   peeled
> 1 celery stalk, cut into chunks
> 1 orange, sliced but not peeled

Preheat oven to 325°F. Place duck on a roasting rack in a large pan.

In a small mixing bowl, stir together the salt, pepper, rosemary, and butter. Baste the duck inside and out with half of the butter mixture.

In a separate mixing bowl, combine the onion, apple, celery, and orange. Stuff the fruit and vegetable mixture into the cavity of the duck.

Roast the duck for 30 minutes, then baste with remaining butter mixture. Roast for an additional hour, basting occasionally with the drippings and juices in the pan. Discard the stuffed contents of the duck before serving.

☞ *Nor love, nor honor, wealth, nor power,*
Can give the heart a cheerful hour
When health is lost. Be timely wise;
With health all taste of pleasure flies.

JOHN GAY

→PARTY PHEASANT←

European pheasant breeds began to be introduced to North America in the 1730s, and a large number of Chinese pheasants were released here in the 1880s. Pheasants soon populated every part of the continent where there were sufficient trees and foliage for cover. Pheasant meat was considered a delicacy for pioneers who were lucky enough to catch or shoot one.

1 cleaned and aged pheasant (see "Preparing Game Birds," page 53), cut into pieces
1 cup sour cream
½ cup apple cider
1½ tablespoons Worcestershire sauce
¾ teaspoon salt
2 tablespoons minced onion
2 tablespoons minced garlic
½ cup sliced mushrooms
paprika

Preheat oven to 350ºF. Arrange the pheasant pieces in a baking dish.

In a mixing bowl, stir all other ingredients together except the paprika. Pour the mixture over the pheasant pieces, then sprinkle paprika on top. Bake for 1 to 1½ hours or until the meat is very tender, stirring occasionally.

 *The way of the pioneer is always rough.*

HARVEY S. FIRESTONE

Soups
and Stews

Grandma's Apron

When I used to visit Grandma, I was very much impressed
By her all-purpose apron and the power it possessed.
Dear Grandma chose one every day to go right with her dress.
The strings were tied and freshly washed, and maybe even pressed.
As simple the apron was, you never thought about
All the things she used it for that made it look worn out.
She used it for a basket when she gathered up the eggs,
And flapped it as a weapon when hens pecked her feet and legs.
She used it to carry kindling when she stoked the kitchen fire,
And to hold a load of laundry, or to wipe the clothesline wire.
She used it for a hot pad to remove a steaming pan,
And when her brow was heated, she used it for a fan.
It dried our childish tears when we'd scrape a knee and cry,
And made a hiding place when the little ones were shy.
Farm produce took in season in the summer, spring, and fall,
Found its way into the kitchen from Grandma's carryall.
When Grandma went to heaven, God said she now could rest.
I'm sure the apron she chose that day was her Sunday best.

AUTHOR UNKNOWN

+BRUNSWICK STEW+

This chicken stew is thought to have originated in Brunswick County, Virginia, in the early 1800s. The original recipe called for a squirrel tail.

1½ cups fresh or frozen lima beans
1½ cups fresh or frozen corn
1½ cups chicken broth
1 pound chicken, cooked and diced
3 cups chopped tomatoes
2 large onions, chopped
3 potatoes, cooked, peeled, and
    chopped
2 cups water
dash of pepper, garlic, brown sugar,
    and salt
cooking oil
hot sauce to taste

Heat 2 tablespoons oil in a large pot, then add chopped onions. Cook until onions turn clear, then add remaining ingredients.

Simmer the stew for about 20 minutes, stirring occasionally.

+TEXAS CHILI+

The dying words of Kit Carson were "Wish I had time for just one more bowl of chili." In 1977, the Texas state legislature proclaimed chili the official state food of Texas.

2 pounds ground beef
1 pound dried pinto beans
6 cups beef broth (see page 60)
1 green bell pepper, diced
1 onion, diced
3 tablespoons vegetable oil
3 tablespoons chili powder
2 tablespoons flour
2 teaspoons ground cumin
1 tablespoon dried oregano
2 teaspoons salt
¼ teaspoon pepper

Rinse the pinto beans and remove any debris. In a large pot of water, boil the beans until soft (about 3 hours). Drain the beans, remove them from the pot, and set them aside.

In the pot, sauté vegetables and beef in the oil until beef is browned. Add the remaining ingredients; simmer for 45 to 60 minutes.

⟶BEEF BROTH⟵

People of the pioneer era didn't waste anything, and a common place for meat and vegetable scraps was in broths, which were later used in soups.

> 3 to 4 pounds beef scraps (bones
>   included if you have them)
> ¼ pound onion scraps and chunks
>   (not the outer peel)
> ½ pound celery scraps (the ends and
>   so forth)
> ½ pound carrot scraps (peels, ends,
>   and older carrots)
> approximately 12 quarts water

Preheat oven to 400°F. In a large pan, roast the beef scraps in the oven for about 1 hour.

Fill a large stockpot about halfway with water. Stir in the roasted beef scraps, along with the onion, celery, and carrot scraps.

Simmer over low heat for 6 to 8 hours, adding more water as needed to keep the pot full. Strain the broth through a colander to remove the large chunks, then through a cheesecloth or a fine mesh strainer to remove the tiny pieces of scraps.

Return the broth to the pot and cook on medium-high heat until the broth is reduced to about half.

⟶BORSCHT⟵

Originating in the Ukraine, borscht spread to many regions in and around Russia. The soup was brought to America by Eastern European immigrants.

> 1 pound beef steak, cubed
> ½ cup red kidney beans
> 2 garlic cloves, minced
> 1 onion, chopped
> 1 large beet (greens and all), peeled
>   and sliced
> 6 mushrooms, sliced
> 1½ cups shredded cabbage
> 1 cup thinly sliced celery
> 1 cup thinly sliced carrots
> 1 large potato (whole or cut in half)
> 1 cup sour cream

½ cup white vinegar
1½ tablespoons sugar
salt and pepper, to taste

Put the meat and vegetables into a large pot of water. Bring to a boil over medium heat and cook until the beans are tender.

Remove the potato from the soup and place in a mixing bowl. Mash the potato together with the sour cream, vinegar, and sugar.

Put the mashed potato mixture back into the soup and cook another 3 to 5 minutes.

→TRADITIONAL BEEF STEW←

Stew is a soup-like meal with cooked solids and a liquid that forms a type of gravy. A frugal but hearty dish, beef stew was popular among Western European immigrants. When beef was not available, mutton was often used.

1 pound beef chunks
1 large potato, cut into chunks
1 tablespoon oil
2 cups water
1 tablespoon Worcestershire sauce
1 garlic clove
1 bay leaf
½ onion
1 teaspoon salt
¼ teaspoon paprika
¼ teaspoon pepper
dash of ground allspice
2 large carrots, sliced
2 celery ribs, sliced
2 tablespoons cornstarch

In a pot, brown the beef in the oil, then add all ingredients except for the carrots, celery, and cornstarch. Cover and simmer for 60 to 90 minutes.

Stir in the celery and carrots, then cover again and cook for 30 minutes.

Remove a small bowl of liquid from the pot and whisk the cornstarch into it, then pour it back into the stew. Continue cooking another 10 to 15 minutes.

⇥CHICKEN BROTH⇤

Making chicken broth for soups and other recipes was a good way to use leftover chicken bones. The pioneers often fed chicken broth to the sick, believing it had healing properties.

1 pound leftover bones and skin
    from a cooked or raw chicken
2 celery stalks (or 2 cups celery
    scraps)
2 large carrots, cut into large chunks
    (or carrot peels and ends)
1 large onion, cut into large
    segments
10 to 12 cups water
1 teaspoon salt
¼ teaspoon cracked pepper

In a large stockpot, bring all ingredients to a boil, then reduce heat and let simmer for about 4 hours. Occasionally skim the foam off of the top and stir. You also may need to add more water from time to time.

Remove the bones and strain the stock, then return the stock to the pan and continue cooking it until it reaches the desired concentration.

⇥CREAMY CHICKEN SOUP⇤

Chicken soup was brought to America from all over the globe. Almost every wave of settlers made some type of chicken soup. Traditionally, it was made by boiling old, tough chickens that couldn't be eaten otherwise.

3 pounds raw chicken, cubed
8 cups water
1 tablespoon salt
4 peppercorns
2 carrots, sliced
2 celery stalks, sliced
2 cups cream
1 tablespoon butter
1 tablespoon cornstarch

In a large stockpot, stir all ingredients together. Cook over medium heat for about 45 minutes, or until all of the chicken is cooked throughout and the soup is smooth and creamy.

⇢CHICKEN NOODLE SOUP⇠

When the pioneers used chicken broth to treat the common cold, they were on the right track, since modern medicine has proven that the vapors from chicken broth can help clear the nasal passages. The addition of noodles and vegetables to the broth made it more filling and nutritious. Chicken noodle soup is still an extremely popular comfort food, especially on cold days.

3 cups chicken chunks
6 cups chicken broth (see page 62)
6 cups water
2 large carrots, sliced
2 large celery ribs, sliced
½ onion, diced
1 tablespoon chopped fresh parsley
1½ teaspoons salt
1 teaspoon garlic salt
½ teaspoon dried oregano
¼ teaspoon pepper
1½ cups prepackaged or homemade
    noodles (see page 98)
3 tablespoons cornstarch

In a large stockpot, stir all ingredients together except the noodles and cornstarch. Boil the soup for about 10 minutes. Reduce heat to medium low and let soup cook for about 20 minutes, or until the chicken chunks are fully cooked.

Remove a small bowl of liquid and whisk into it the cornstarch, then pour it back into the soup. Gently stir in the noodles and let cook another 5 to 10 minutes, or just until the noodles are done.

☞ *A woman can throw out more with a spoon than a man can bring in with a shovel.*

→SWEDISH CABBAGE SOUP WITH MEATBALLS←

This authentic soup begins with stock made from lamb. However, if canned beef stock is used, the soup can be prepared in only 30 minutes. There are a number of variations of this soup in the United States, due to the assimilation of Swedish immigrants in the Midwest.

2 to 4 pounds lamb stew meat or
   lamb flank
1 celery stalk, including leaves, cut
   in chunks
1 carrot, cut in chunks
salt to taste
whole peppercorns to taste
2 or 3 allspice berries
1 large green cabbage, cut into bite-
   size pieces
1 pound ground chuck
1 egg
½ small onion, finely chopped
1 teaspoon salt (or less)
¼ teaspoon pepper

Cover the lamb with cold water in a large saucepan or stockpot. Add the celery and carrot. Bring to a boil and simmer for about 4 hours, removing the foam that forms on top. Remove the meat and reserve for another use. Refrigerate broth overnight to allow the fat to harden and rise to the surface.

The next day, skim the fat off the broth. Add salt and peppercorns to taste, along with the allspice berries and cabbage. Cover and simmer on low heat for 15 minutes.

To make the meatballs, combine the ground chuck, egg, onion, salt, and pepper. Form into very small meatballs. Bring soup to a boil and drop the meatballs one by one into the boiling soup. Cover and simmer for another 15 to 20 minutes.

For a heartier variation, add 1 cup fine egg noodles 5 minutes before serving.

☞ *People who boil and stew will cook in their own juices.*

⇥PACIFIC COAST CLAM CHOWDER⇤

Immigrants from coastal England and France brought fish-milk stew to America, where the natives replaced the fish with clams to make what became known as clam chowder. Classic New England-style clam chowder traditionally begins with salt pork or bacon. The Pacific Coast version is similar, but in Seattle and Portland, smoked salmon is often added to the chowder in place of bacon. The following recipe is from Linda Stradley (whatscookingamerica.net).

> 5 bacon slices, cut into ¼-inch
>   pieces
> ¼ cup (½ stick butter)
> 1 medium onion, chopped
> ¼ cup all-purpose flour
> salt and pepper, to taste
> 4 cups milk
> potatoes, peeled and cut into ¼-inch
>   pieces (amount to taste)
> two 6.5-ounce cans minced clams,
>   undrained

Boil potatoes in a large pot until they are soft. Drain water. Place potatoes in a bowl and set aside.

In a large soup pot over medium heat, sauté bacon until crisp. Remove bacon with a slotted spoon and drain on paper towels. Remove bacon fat from soup pot. Set bacon aside.

Reduce heat to low and add butter. Stir until melted. Add onions and cook until they are translucent and soft (about 10 to 15 minutes).

Whisk in the flour, salt, and pepper until well blended. Gradually add milk, stirring constantly until sauce comes to a boil and thickens.

Add potatoes and clams and heat through. Serve with bread or crackers.

☞ *First thrive and then wive.*

⇥FISH CHOWDER⇤

Fish chowder is a well-known dish passed down to us from French, French Canadian, and British pioneers who spent a great deal of time on boats before they made the treks to their final destinations.

     4 pounds white fish meat (any kind),
         cut into cubes
     5 potatoes, cut into cubes
     1 large onion, diced
     1 tablespoon salt
     ½ teaspoon pepper
     1 tablespoon butter
     1 tablespoon flour
     4 cups milk
     juice of 1 lemon (optional)
     2 cloves garlic, minced or chopped

Stir all ingredients together in a soup pot. Boil for about half an hour or until the potatoes are tender.

☞ *An apple never falls far from the tree.*

⇥CHEESE SOUP⇤

This type of soup has been handed down to us from our French and Canadian pioneers.

     ½ onion, chopped
     ¼ cup butter
     ¼ cup flour
     1½ tablespoons cornstarch
     ½ teaspoon paprika
     ½ teaspoon salt
     ¼ teaspoon pepper
     4 cups milk
     4 cups chicken or vegetable broth
     ½ cup sliced carrots
     ½ cup sliced celery
     ½ cup broccoli florets, cut small
     1 cup grated cheddar cheese
     2 to 3 tablespoons chopped fresh
         parsley

In a soup pot, sauté the onions in the butter for about 3 minutes over medium heat.

Add the flour, cornstarch, paprika, salt, and pepper. Mix well with a whisk, then pour in the milk and broth.

Stir in the cut vegetables and continue cooking until they are tender (10 to 15 minutes).

Stir in the cheese and parsley. The soup is done when the cheese is completely melted and incorporated into the soup.

+VEGETABLE BROTH+

Vegetable broth can be used as the base for almost any soup. This inexpensive broth can also be used to thin or add flavor to sauces and gravies. Just remember to save your vegetable scraps!

> 3 pounds vegetable scraps (any
> mixture of older vegetables,
> scraps, skins, and ends)
> 2 teaspoons salt
> ½ teaspoon cracked pepper
> approximately 12 quarts water

Put the vegetable scraps, salt, and water in a large stockpot. Fill the pot with water. Simmer for about an hour, then strain out the chunks and small pieces of vegetables.

+PUMPKIN SOUP+

The first pumpkin soup was created in Haiti in 1804 to celebrate the country's independence from France. Pumpkin soup is still very popular in Haiti around Independence Day (January 1), and in the United States during the fall season.

> 6 cups chicken broth (see page 62)
> 4 cups cooked pumpkin purée
> ½ cup heavy cream
> ½ cup chopped onion
> 2 to 3 garlic cloves, minced
> 1 teaspoon chopped parsley
> 1½ teaspoons salt
> ½ teaspoon chopped thyme
> ½ teaspoon ground nutmeg
> ¼ teaspoon pepper

In a large pot, combine all ingredients and cook over medium heat, stirring occasionally, until all of the flavors are well combined (about 20 minutes).

☞ *The past is a bucket of ashes.*

ꜛVEGETABLE SOUPꜜ

To make vegetable soup, pioneers simply threw whatever they had from the garden, or could forage, into a large pot of water and added seasonings. Delicious!

> 1 large slice of bacon (optional)
> 3 cups diced tomatoes (canned is fine)
> 1 cup fresh or frozen corn
> 1 cup chopped cabbage
> 1 cup lima beans
> 1 large potato, cubed
> 1 turnip, sliced
> 1 carrot, sliced
> ¼ cup chopped onion
> 2 tablespoons chopped fresh parsley
> 1 teaspoon salt
> ½ teaspoon pepper
> 1½ tablespoons flour
> ½ cup milk

If using bacon, boil it in a large pot of water for at least 30 minutes, then add remaining ingredients except flour and milk. If not using bacon, place all ingredients except flour and milk in a large pot of water.

In a small mixing bowl, whisk the milk and flour together, then stir into the soup. Boil about 1 hour or until all of the vegetables are tender.

ꜛKIDNEY BEAN STEWꜜ

Kidney beans originated near Peru and were taken to the rest of the world by Indian traders. By the 17th century, kidney beans had reached the British colonies in America, where they became an important source of protein.

> 2 pounds dried kidney beans
> 3 potatoes, peeled and cubed
> 4 large carrots
> 6 cups beef broth (see page 60) or vegetable broth (see page 67)
> 8 cups water
> ½ onion, chopped
> 3 teaspoons salt
> 2 teaspoons garlic powder
> 1 teaspoon onion powder
> 1 bay leaf
> ½ teaspoon sage

Place the beans in a large stockpot, cover with water, and bring to a boil. Boil for 10 minutes, then drain the water.

Stir in the remaining ingredients, cover the pot, and cook over medium heat, stirring occasionally, for 5 to 6 hours, or until the beans are tender.

⁺PEA SOUP⁺

For centuries, variations of pea soup have been eaten in many different cultures around the world. Depending on the type of pea used, the soup is either yellow or light green in color. French Canadian millworkers introduced pea soup to New Englanders in the 19th century, where the dish is still quite popular.

    4 cups dried English peas
    4 quarts water
    6 peppercorns
    2 cloves garlic, chopped
    1 large onion, chopped
    2 or 3 potatoes, diced
    salt to taste

    1 tablespoon sage (optional)
    1 tablespoon thyme (optional)
    2 tablespoons lovage (optional)

Place all ingredients except potatoes in a large soup pot and bring to a boil. Skim off any foam that rises to the top. Simmer until peas are almost cooked, adding more water if they start to stick to the pot.

Add potatoes and cook until they are soft. Serve with johnny cakes or biscuits.

☞ *A stomach that is seldom empty despises common food.*

HORACE

→NOVA SCOTIAN HODGEPODGE←

Hodgepodge, or as the British say, hodgepotch, is a random assortment or mixture, so the name fits well for a stew made with various types of vegetables. Vegetable stews date back to at least the 1400s. This particular recipe is an old favorite from Nova Scotia that was typically made in the fall just as gardens were harvested.

1 cup fresh green beans, trimmed
    and snapped
1 cup fresh wax beans, trimmed and
    snapped
1 cup diced carrot
1 cup diced turnip
2 cups cubed new potatoes
6 tablespoons butter
½ cup heavy cream (optional)
1 tablespoon all-purpose flour
½ cup water

Place all vegetables in a large pot and add water to cover. Salt the water lightly and bring to a boil. Cook for about 40 minutes. Stir in butter. Add the cream, if desired.

Mix the flour with ½ cup water; pour mixture into the soup. Cook soup for a few more minutes to thicken. Remove soup from heat and serve hot.

→LENTIL STEW←

Lentils have been a food staple for thousands of years. Varieties of lentils include brown, yellow, red, green, and black. Most historians believe that when Esau sold his birthright for pottage, that pottage consisted of a bowl of lentils. The origin of this nutrient-rich legume can be traced back to the Near East. From there, lentil cultivation spread to the Mediterranean regions, Asia, Europe, and finally the Americas in the early 1900s.

1 pound dried lentils
2 cups vegetable broth (see page 67)
5 cups water
¼ cup ground oats, wheat, or flax
½ cup chopped onions
2 carrots, sliced
2 potatoes, cubed
1½ teaspoons salt

1 teaspoon garlic salt
1 teaspoon chopped parsley (dried
   or fresh)
½ teaspoon onion powder
¼ teaspoon pepper

Rinse the lentils, then place them in a large stockpot with the remaining ingredients. Cook over medium heat, stirring occasionally, until all vegetables and lentils are soft (40 to 50 minutes).

→POTATO SOUP←

The earliest civilization to cultivate and enjoy the potato in all of its varieties was located in what we now call Peru. When the Spanish conquistadors raided Peru looking for gold, they found none but settled for potatoes. Over the next few centuries, potatoes spread all over Europe and consequently to the plains and frontier settlements of the United States.

3 large potatoes, cubed
4 cups milk
1 cup water

¼ cup chopped onion
1 celery stalk, sliced
1 tablespoon butter
1½ teaspoons salt
¼ teaspoon pepper
¼ teaspoon cayenne pepper

In a soup pot, combine all ingredients and cook over medium heat. Stir occasionally and let boil for 30 to 45 minutes or until the potatoes are completely tender. Slightly mash the potatoes to thicken the soup.

☞ *Reach for the high apples first, you can get the lower ones any time.*

→TOMATO SOUP←

Even though tomato soup originated in South America, it was the European settlers and pioneers, particularly the French, that made it popular in the continental U.S.

2 cups diced tomatoes
4 cups water
1 tablespoon sugar
1 teaspoon salt
4 cloves
4 peppercorns
¼ cup chopped onion
2 tablespoons chopped fresh parsley
1 tablespoon butter
1 tablespoon cornstarch

In a soup pot, combine the water, tomatoes, sugar, salt, cloves, and peppercorns, and begin cooking on medium heat.

In a separate pan, cook the onion and parsley in the butter for a few minutes over medium heat, then whisk in the cornstarch. Pour mixture into the cooking soup. Boil another 30 to 45 minutes, mashing the tomatoes as you stir occasionally.

→FRUIT SOUP←

Fruit soup, or frukt soppa, *was brought to America by Swedish settlers. You can use any berry in place of the cherries, but pioneers typically used rose hip (the fruit of a rose, especially the wild kind) or bilberries (similar to blueberries).*

4 cups water
2 cups cherries, pitted
1 large apple, cored and cut into
    chunks, but not peeled
1 orange, sliced but not peeled
1 lemon, sliced but not peeled
1 cup raisins
1 cup sugar
½ teaspoon salt
½ cup tapioca
whipped cream

In a pot, boil all ingredients except the tapioca and whipped cream over medium heat for about 25 minutes. Stir in the tapioca and boil another 12 to 14 minutes. Serve the soup warm or cool with whipped cream on top.

☞ *Thank Heaven for small favors.*

Sauces and
Dressings

Just as the New Year Was Dawning

Just as the new year was dawning
His mind wandered back to the past
Friends of his youth passed before him,
Would that those visions might last.

Tired and calm he lay resting,
And quietly soon fell asleep,
And thus as he watched by the bedside
He silently passed o'er the deep.

The pioneer band is fast passing
Yet their spirit will linger for aye,
The work and foundation they builded
Was not made to crumble away;

But will stand as a monument to them,
And their brave dauntless spirit of old.
The true heart, the quick hand, the kindness
Are to us far dearer than gold.

ELIZABETH MCGRATH

→WHITE SAUCE←

The versatile white sauce was used by pioneers in a variety of meals. It was used as a gravy starter, to make soups creamy, and as a moist component in early casseroles.

1½ cups milk
2 tablespoons butter
3 tablespoons flour
½ teaspoon salt
¼ teaspoon pepper

Whisk all ingredients together. Cook over medium heat in a small saucepan for 3 to 5 minutes, or until sauce thickens.

→BROWN GRAVY←

In pioneer days, brown gravy was often used at mealtime to flavor and moisten meats and potatoes.

2 cups meat broth (from boiling any kind of meat)

2 tablespoons butter
3 tablespoons flour
½ teaspoon salt
¼ teaspoon pepper

In a small saucepan over medium heat, cook the butter and broth until the butter melts.

Whisk in the remaining ingredients, then bring to a boil. Boil the liquid for about 1 minute, stirring constantly.

Remove from heat and let stand a few minutes before serving.

☞ *The world is your cow, but you have to do the milking.*

⇥BUTTER SAUCE⇤

This sauce was often served over cooked fish or other seafood.

> 2 cups hot water
> ½ cup butter
> 2 tablespoons flour
> ½ teaspoon salt
> ¼ teaspoon pepper

In a saucepan over medium heat, melt half of the butter. Whisk in the water, flour, salt, and pepper.

⇥LEMON BUTTER SAUCE⇤

This sauce is perfect for seafood and poultry.

> butter sauce (recipe above)
> juice from 1 lemon
> 1 teaspoon lemon zest

Just after the butter sauce is made and while it is still being heated, stir in the lemon juice and zest. Stir and cook for about 1 minute.

When the mixture is smooth, add the remaining butter and stir until all is melted and well combined.

⇥HORSERADISH SAUCE⇤

Horseradish sauce originated in Eastern Europe and was most commonly used to flavor meat.

> 1½ cups sour cream
> ⅓ cup grated horseradish root
> 1½ tablespoons Dijon mustard
> 1½ teaspoons vinegar
> ¾ teaspoon salt
> ⅓ teaspoon black pepper

Whisk all ingredients together in a mixing bowl until smooth and creamy. Refrigerate for at least 2 hours before serving.

☞ *Don't fall out with your bread and butter.*

→ONION SAUCE←

Onion sauce was served with meat, including wild game, and added to stews.

> 4 large onions (outer skin peeled
>   off)
> ¾ cup milk
> 1 tablespoon flour
> 1 teaspoon salt
> ¼ teaspoon pepper
> 1 teaspoon Tabasco sauce (optional)
> 2 tablespoons butter

In a pot of salted water, boil the onions until tender. Remove the onions from the water and chop them finely.

In a saucepan over medium heat, whisk together the milk, flour, salt, and pepper. Add the onions and butter (and Tabasco sauce if using). Stir until the butter is melted and the sauce is well combined.

☞ *Beauty cannot compensate for want of heart.*

→KETCHUP←

British and Dutch sailors brought "ketsiap" to Europe from China in the 1600s. It made its way to the Americas, like so many culinary favorites, along with the colonial settlers. The recipe has evolved a great deal the past few centuries. This version is popular in the United States today.

> 3 large tomatoes
> 1 medium onion
> 2 tablespoons olive oil
> 1 tablespoon flour
> ⅔ cup brown sugar, firmly packed
> ½ cup cider vinegar
> ½ teaspoon salt

Purée the tomatoes and onion in a food processor or blender.

In a skillet, whisk all ingredients together and cook over medium heat for about 30 minutes.

Pour into a jar or covered dish. Refrigerate for at least 3 hours before serving.

→CRANBERRY SAUCE←

This sauce was traditionally served with ham or any type of bird in the winter.

1 cup water
1 cup sugar
2 cups whole cranberries

In a saucepan, bring the water and sugar to a boil over medium heat.

Stir in the cranberries and reduce heat. Let the sauce cook for about 10 minutes, stirring constantly.

Remove from heat, put into a jar or covered dish, cover, and refrigerate for at least 6 hours before serving.

→APPLE BUTTER←

Apple butter was created in Germany and was known as cider-boiled applesauce. It became a favorite spread for bread and muffins all over the American colonies, especially among the Pennsylvanian Dutch. The name was changed to apple butter in Appalachia.

4 pounds Granny Smith or
    Gravenstein apples
1 cup apple cider vinegar
3 cups sugar
2 teaspoons ground cinnamon
½ teaspoon ground cloves
½ teaspoon ground allspice
½ teaspoon salt
juice of 1 lemon
1 teaspoon grated lemon rind

Core the apples (leave the peel on), and purée them in a food processor or blender.

Stir all ingredients together in a large, wide-mouthed pot or skillet. Stir often, remembering to scrape the bottom of the pot when you stir, and cook over medium heat for about an hour, or until a smooth, thick consistency is reached.

This recipe may be used for canning. Simply pour the hot apple butter into sterilized jars, wipe the brim of the jars clean, and cover with sterilized lids.

→PUMPKIN BUTTER←

Pumpkin was a staple crop of Native Americans, and early colonial settlers learned to depend on it as well. The following old verse is illustrative of this fact: "For pottage, and puddings, and custards, and pies, Our pumpkins and parsnips are common supplies. We have pumpkins at morning and pumpkins at noon; If it were not for pumpkins, we should be undoon." This pumpkin butter spread is very good on breads and muffins.

1½ cups cooked pumpkin purée
1½ cups sugar
¾ cups apple juice
2 teaspoons ground ginger
2 teaspoons ground cinnamon
1 teaspoon ground nutmeg
¼ teaspoon ground cloves

Stir all ingredients together in a large skillet. Bring to a boil, then reduce heat and simmer, stirring frequently, for about 30 minutes, or until the pumpkin butter becomes thick. Let cool to room temperature before serving.

Pumpkin butter may be stored in the refrigerator for up to a month, or in the freezer for 6 months.

→HONEY BUTTER←

As a condiment, honey butter is a fairly modern invention. Centuries ago, it was used as a medicine to treat tuberculosis and consumption. Honey butter is an excellent spread for muffins, biscuits, and bread.

½ cup butter, at room temperature
½ cup honey

In a mixing bowl, whip together the butter and honey until smooth and combined well. Serve at room temperature.

☞ *If bees stay at home,*
rain will soon come;
If they fly away,
fine will be the day.

→CRACKED-PEPPER BUTTERMILK SALAD DRESSING←

The old-fashioned way to crack peppercorns is to wrap up as many as you need in a tea towel, place it on a counter or very hard work surface (even the ground or pavement), and whack the wrapped peppercorns repeatedly with a heavy cast-iron skillet.

1 cup buttermilk
1 cup mayonnaise
¼ cup finely chopped parsley
1 teaspoon cracked pepper
½ teaspoon salt
½ teaspoon garlic powder

In a small bowl, whisk all ingredients together until well blended.

☞ *"To make a salad dressing, four persons are wanted: A spendthrift, for oil; a miser, for vinegar; a counselor, for salt; and a madman to stir it up."*

SPANISH PROVERB

→RASPBERRY VINAIGRETTE←

The word vinaigrette *comes from the French word for aromatic vinegar, which is* vinaigre. *According to dictionary.reference.com, the term* vinaigrette *was coined between 1690 and 1700. However, as a reference to a dressing for salads or cold vegetables, the word* vinaigrette *probably originated in about 1877 (see www.etymonline. com). Pioneers wouldn't have had access to olive oil, but it is called for here because it is healthier than other cooking oils. However, wild raspberries were often available to pioneers, and vinegar was a staple ingredient in pioneer cooking.*

¼ cup puréed raspberries
¼ cup olive oil
2½ tablespoons apple cider vinegar
1 teaspoon salt
½ teaspoon ground oregano
¼ teaspoon cracked pepper

Whisk the ingredients together in a bowl, then toss with salad greens.

Side Dishes

Dedicated to the Boys Who Crossed the Plains with Me in 1852

Comrades, it is growing late, 'tis camping time,
Here let us rest on the banks of this stream;
Yonder is a spring, and wood to light our fire by;
Green pastures on every hand to rest our jaded team.

Yes, let us gather 'round the fire once again;
For we must be nearing our journey's end;
The plains are past, the mountains are in view,
The slope beyond where sky and water blend.

How like life the overland journey seems
The plains the morning, ere the noon begins;
The mountains gained, snow-capped we find
Morning past, the evening tide appears.

Comrades, our journey o'er the plains is nearly done,
The golden shore lies just beyond;
Our fire is burning low—another day begun;
We may reach there ere night comes on.

SAMUEL HARDEN, MAY 1887

→HOPPIN' JOHN←

Hoppin' john is a simple yet hearty dish that was popular on the trail and in pioneer kitchens.

1½ cups black-eyed peas
1 onion, chopped
1 bell pepper, diced
1 teaspoon salt
½ teaspoon pepper
¼ teaspoon crushed red pepper
3 tablespoons vegetable oil,
    or 8 ounces bacon, cut into
    small pieces
3 cups steamed rice

Rinse the peas, then soak them overnight in a large pot of water. Bring the peas to a boil and add vegetables and seasonings. Reduce heat slightly, cover, and cook for an hour.

In a separate skillet, fry the bacon if using. Put the bacon and drippings into the pea mixture and continue to cook for another 45 minutes. If not using bacon, stir in the oil at this point.

When the peas are very soft, try to mash them (not the vegetables or bacon, just the peas). Serve over steamed rice.

→SUCCOTASH←

This recipe has been handed down from the pioneers who came from New England. The dish was taught to the colonial settlers by Native Americans.

2 cups fresh or frozen lima beans
1 cup fresh or frozen corn
½ cup milk
½ cup butter
2 tomatoes, diced
salt and pepper, to taste
dash of nutmeg

In a skillet over medium heat, melt the butter with the milk. Add the lima beans and corn. Cook until tender, then stir in the tomatoes and seasonings.

☞ *When frogs holler, rain will soon foller.*

→FRIED GREEN TOMATOES←

Most people assume that fried green tomatoes originated in the southern United States, but they were actually enjoyed in Italy in the 16th century. And in America, fried green tomatoes first became popular in the Northeast. After an early frost, some New England farmers, tired of feeding their unripened tomatoes to their animals, decided to coat the green tomatoes with a batter and fry them. According to thestrongbuzz.com, the first published American reference to frying green tomatoes appeared in the New England Farmer *in 1835. The idea spread to the Midwest and more particularly to the South, where fried green tomatoes are a staple in many homes.*

2 large green tomatoes
1 egg
¼ cup milk
½ cup flour
¼ cup cornmeal
¼ cup breadcrumbs
1 teaspoon salt
¼ teaspoon cracked pepper
⅛ teaspoon cayenne pepper
   (optional)
oil for frying

Slice the tomatoes ½ inch thick. In a small bowl, whisk together the egg and milk.

Place the flour on a small plate. On another plate, combine the cornmeal, breadcrumbs, salt, pepper, and cayenne pepper, mixing well.

Pour oil in a large skillet until the oil is ½ inch deep. Heat the oil on medium heat.

Dip both sides of each tomato slice in the flour, then the milk–egg mixture, then the cornmeal mixture. Fry tomatoes in the hot oil in batches, making sure the slices do not touch each other. Once the bottom of each slice is golden brown, carefully flip it and cook the other side, about 4 to 7 minutes each side. Drain on paper towels.

⇢FRIED OKRA⇠

Wild okra was first discovered on the banks of the Nile in Egypt. The vegetable gradually made its way through Africa and then up through the Mediterranean and India. During the slave trade, okra was brought to New Orleans, and it soon became a staple of the South. Okra is used most commonly in soups, such as gumbo, and fried, as in this recipe.

> canola or vegetable oil for frying
> 2 pounds fresh okra, cut into ½-inch
>   segments
> ½ cup buttermilk
> ½ cup cornmeal
> ½ cup flour
> 1 teaspoon salt
> ½ teaspoon garlic powder
> ¼ teaspoon pepper
> ⅛ teaspoon cayenne pepper

Fill a skillet about ⅓ deep with cooking oil. Heat over medium to medium-high heat. In a mixing bowl, whisk together the cornmeal, flour, salt, garlic powder, pepper, and cayenne pepper. Set aside.

Dip each okra piece in the buttermilk, then quickly coat in the cornmeal mixture. Carefully place the okra in the hot oil and stir gently while cooking. When each side is golden brown and slightly crispy, remove the okra from the oil and place it on paper towels to dry. Serve immediately.

⇢BRUSSELS SPROUTS⇠

These are very miniature cabbages that originated in Northern Europe and were brought to America by French settlers.

> Brussels sprouts
> melted butter or gravy
> salt and pepper, to taste

Steam Brussels sprouts, then serve with melted butter or gravy and salt and pepper.

☞ *Oh, it will pass with a shove, if you shove hard enough.*

⋆SAUTÉED ZUCCHINI⋆

Zucchini, a type of summer squash, is native to the Americas. In the area we now know as Mexico, zucchini was eaten as early as 7000 B.C. European explorers brought zucchini squash to Europe, where it was named zucchini *or* zucchino *by the Italians.*

1 large or 2 medium zucchini
3 tablespoons olive oil
3 tablespoons water
¼ teaspoon salt
¼ teaspoon garlic salt
¼ teaspoon onion powder
⅛ teaspoon pepper

Stir all ingredients together in a frying pan and cook over medium heat, stirring frequently, until the zucchini is just tender but not limp.

☞ *The only church we ever knew was around our mother's knees.*

STEPHEN M. WHITE

⋆VEGETABLE FRITTERS⋆

Fritters are popular in many different cultures around the world. This type of fritter, where vegetables are coated with a batter and deep fried, was made by Native Americans, who typically used corn in their fritters. Early colonists picked up the idea and made fritters with just about any cooked vegetable they had on hand. The following is adapted from a recipe by Patricia B. Mitchell in The Good Land: Native American and Early Colonial Food *(rev. ed. [Chatham, VA: Mitchells Publications, 2007]).*

1 cup flour
1 teaspoon baking powder
½ teaspoon salt
1 egg
½ cup milk
1 teaspoon melted butter
1 cup cooked, chopped vegetables
    (carrots, corn, peas, green beans,
    mushrooms, etc.), drained
vegetable oil for cooking (about 1
    cup)

Sift together flour, baking powder, and salt. Beat egg, then add milk and butter. Add to flour mixture and beat until smooth. Add vegetables.

Pour oil into a skillet and heat on medium-high heat. When oil is hot, drop batter by tablespoons into skillet. Fry until fritters are well browned on both sides, about 4 minutes total. Drain fritters on paper towels.

⤑SAUTÉED ASPARAGUS⤐

Asparagus is native to many coastal areas in Europe, Asia, and Africa. The versatile vegetable was brought to North America by early settlers, and it has been cultivated in home gardens ever since. Wild asparagus still grows along the banks of many rivers and creeks in North America.

> 20 to 25 asparagus stalks
> 1 or 2 garlic cloves, minced
> 3 tablespoons water
> 2 tablespoons olive oil
> ½ teaspoon salt
> ¼ teaspoon cracked pepper

Stir all ingredients together in a large skillet. Cover and cook over medium heat, stirring occasionally, until the asparagus is tender and the water is cooked out.

⤑BOILED CABBAGE⤐

Boiled cabbage was a typical side vegetable served with meat and bread in New England as well as on the frontier. Usually it was boiled in a large pot with either corned beef (see page 18), or homemade sausage (see page 32). Here is a simple recipe for boiled cabbage.

> 1 head cabbage
> 3 tablespoons butter or olive oil

Cut the head of cabbage into large segments, then boil in a large pot of salted water with the oil or butter. The cabbage will be soft enough to eat after boiling for 12 to 15 minutes.

→COLLARD GREENS←

Collard greens were fed to slaves on Southern plantations and were prepared in large pots. Everything was eaten, including all of the liquid, to nourish the large families. When the slaves were brought into the kitchen to cook, they would often make dishes familiar to them, such as collard greens.

>   2 large bundles of collard leaves
>   1 ham hock
>   salt to taste

In a large pot, cover the ham hock with water and boil at least 30 minutes.

Wash, trim, and chop the collard greens, then add them to the pot. Cook until the leaves are tender. Add salt to taste.

☞ *Eat an apple going to bed, knock the doctor on the head.*

→MASHED BANANA SQUASH←

Banana squash is native to South America. As they migrated north, Native Americans brought this winter squash (meaning it is picked when it is ripe) with them. By the time of the American Revolution, banana squash was cultivated by Native American tribes throughout North America.

>   4-inch-thick slice of banana squash,
>   seeds and innards removed
>   3 tablespoons brown sugar
>   2 tablespoons butter
>   salt and pepper, to taste

Preheat oven to 400°F. Place the slice of banana squash on a cookie sheet. Bake for 40 to 50 minutes, or until the flesh of the squash is very tender and easily mashed with a fork.

Remove the hard shell from the squash. In a large bowl, mash together the squash flesh, brown sugar, and butter. Add salt and pepper to taste.

→TURNIP GREENS←

Turnips came to the Americas by way of early European colonists and settlers. Turnips grew well in the South and became popular on plantations. Many plantation owners would keep the turnips for themselves and give the leaves or "greens" to their slaves.

1 large bundle of turnip greens
1 piece of bacon
salt, to taste

Clean and chop the greens, then boil them in water.

In a skillet, cook the bacon until crisp. Drain the drippings and set aside.

Remove the greens with a strainer and put them in the skillet with the bacon. Stir and cook together for about 5 minutes.

☞ *A maiden's reserve is worth more for her protection than bolts and bars.*

→TURNIP PUFF←

Many early settlers grew large turnips to feed to their animals, plus a smaller, tender version to eat themselves. This recipe makes use of extra turnips from the garden harvest.

4 cups boiled, mashed turnips
4 tablespoons butter
2 teaspoons sugar
1 teaspoon salt
2 eggs, separated
pinch nutmeg
pinch pepper, to taste

Beat together the turnips, butter, sugar, salt, nutmeg, pepper, and egg yolks.

Whip the egg whites until stiff, then fold into the turnip mixture. Place in a buttered 1½ quart casserole dish and bake at 350°F for 15 to 20 minutes.

⇥ROASTED CORN⇤

American settlers learned about corn—and the many ways to cook it—from the Native Americans, who had been cultivating it for centuries before the Europeans arrived.

>   desired number of corn cobs, with
>   husks still on
>   butter
>   salt and pepper, to taste

Heat oven to 350°F. Place the corn cobs (husks and all) directly on the oven rack and bake for 30 to 35 minutes, or until the kernels are soft.

Peel back the husks and slather the corn in butter. Add salt and pepper to taste.

⇥STUFFED ACORN SQUASH⇤

Squash was a staple food of Native Americans, who shared it with early settlers from Europe. Squash is indigenous to Mexico and Central America. It is rumored that Christopher Columbus took squash with him when he returned to Spain. Acorn is a winter squash that is harvested at maturity, generally the end of summer.

>   3 medium acorn squash
>   ½ teaspoon salt
>   3 cups apple, chopped but not
>   peeled
>   ¼ cup butter, melted
>   ½ cup chopped fresh cranberries
>   ¼ cup chopped walnuts
>   ¼ cup brown sugar, firmly packed

Preheat oven to 350°F. Cut the squash in half and remove the seeds and innards. Place the squash on a baking sheet, cut side down, and roast for 30 to 35 minutes.

In a mixing bowl, stir together the chopped apple, melted butter, cranberries, walnuts, and brown sugar.

Turn the roasted squash with the cut side up. Sprinkle the salt over the squash flesh. Fill the pockets with the stuffing. Bake for another 25 to 30 minutes.

→OLD-FASHIONED GREEN BEANS←

Green beans fried with bacon is a traditional Dutch dish. For a complete meal, serve these beans with meat and bread and butter.

2 tablespoons bacon grease
1 pound fresh green beans, cleaned
1½ cups hot beef broth
¼ cup chopped onion
ground black pepper to taste
chopped bacon, if desired

In a large saucepan, heat bacon grease on medium-high heat. Add beans and sauté until bright green. Drain off excess grease.

Add the onion and hot beef broth. Bring to a boil, then reduce heat. Cover and simmer for about an hour. Before serving, add bacon bits and pepper.

☞ *Corn must be knee high by the fourth of July.*

→BOILED POTATOES←

The practice of boiling potatoes dates back several thousand years. Boiled potatoes as an entrée or side dish was as common in pioneer days as it is today. This type of boiled potato recipe was popular among the northeastern American colonies.

1 pound small new or red potatoes
(washed, with skin on)
4 garlic cloves, quartered
1 bay leaf
3 to 4 peppercorns
3 tablespoons butter
salt and pepper, to taste

Place the potatoes, garlic, bay leaf, and peppercorn in a large skillet. Sprinkle with an ample amount of salt. Cover potatoes with water, then place a lid on the pan.

Cook the potatoes over medium heat until they are tender. Drain the water and discard the bay leaf, garlic, and peppercorns.

Toss potatoes with butter, then add salt and pepper to taste.

→MASHED POTATOES←

Even though many European countries, including Ireland and Poland, claim to have "invented" mashed potatoes, they actually originated in the Andes Mountains in South America. The Europeans did, however, bring the dish to the colonies in America. Mashed potatoes have been enjoyed all over the United States for many generations.

> 3 large potatoes, peeled and cut into
> chunks
> ¾ cup cream or milk
> 2 tablespoons butter
> salt and pepper, to taste

In a pot of water, boil the potato chunks until they are very soft. Drain the water. Mash the potatoes, then stir in the remaining ingredients.

☞ *Fine words butter no parsnips.*

→POTATO SALAD←

According to foodtimeline.org, potato salad was introduced to America by European settlers, who adapted traditional foods to local ingredients. British and French immigrants preferred cold potato salads, while German settlers made warm potato salads with bacon drippings and vinegar. As we know it today, potato salad became popular in America in the mid- to late-1800s. The following is a traditional cold potato salad.

> 6 medium potatoes (about 2 pounds)
> ¾ cup chopped sweet pickles (or to
> taste)
> 2 tablespoons chopped onion
> ¾ cup chopped celery
> salt, to taste
> 1½ teaspoons celery seeds
> potato salad dressing
> 6 hard-cooked eggs (5 chopped and
> 1 sliced)
> fresh parsley (optional)
> 2 tablespoons chopped pimiento
> (optional)
> paprika

Potato Salad Dressing

¾ cup mayonnaise
1½ tablespoons prepared mustard
1 teaspoon sugar
1 to 2 tablespoons sweet pickle juice
(or more to taste)

Place potatoes in a large pan and cover with cold water. Bring to a boil, then reduce heat and simmer, uncovered, for 12 to 15 minutes or until just tender. Remove from heat and drain. Let the potatoes cool slightly and cut them into bite-sized chunks. Place in a large mixing bowl.

Add sweet pickles, onion, and celery to the potato chunks. Sprinkle with salt and celery seeds and stir until well blended.

Prepare potato salad dressing by placing all ingredients in a small bowl and combining well. Pour dressing over the potato mixture. Toss gently until well mixed. Gently mix in the chopped hard-cooked egg. Refrigerate salad for several hours.

Place potato salad in a large serving bowl. Garnish with remaining sliced egg and parsley, then sprinkle with paprika. Cover and refrigerate at least 2 hours before serving.

→ROASTED CHESTNUTS→

Settlers from all over Europe brought with them a love of chestnuts. Roasting chestnuts was a winter holiday treat.

Desired amount of chestnuts

Preheat oven to 400°F. Prepare each chestnut by cutting a large X with a paring knife through the skin on the flat side of the nut.

Place the cut nuts on a cookie sheet. Bake for 30 to 40 minutes, stirring the nuts often for even roasting.

Peel the nuts as soon as they are cool enough to handle.

☞ *If a bat bites you, your ears and nose will change places.*

→BAKED BEANS→

This type of sweet bean stew came from France and the Channel Islands. It eventually made its way through England, Ireland, Italy, and then the northern colonies in America. While today's baked beans are usually cooked in large stew pots, they were originally placed in ceramic or cast-iron bean pots that were buried in stone-lined fire pits for several hours.

2 cups navy or great northern beans
¼ pound bacon, diced
1 onion, finely chopped
3 tablespoons molasses
2 teaspoons salt
¼ teaspoon pepper
¼ teaspoon ground mustard
½ cup ketchup
2 tablespoons Worcestershire sauce
¼ cup brown sugar, firmly packed

Soak beans in cold water overnight, then cook them in water over medium heat for 1 to 2 hours, or until they are tender.

Preheat oven to 325°F. Scoop the beans into a large baking dish, reserving the broth, and stir in remaining ingredients. Cover beans with broth. Bake for 3 to 4 hours, stirring occasionally and adding more bean broth if needed to keep the beans saucy.

→GERMAN BAKED BEANS←

While German baked beans often contain sauerkraut, this recipe omits it but retains the traditional ingredients of hamburger and applesauce.

½ pound hamburger
1 small onion, chopped
2 tablespoons butter
3½ cups homemade baked beans, or
    one 28-ounce can
¼ cup catsup
3 tablespoons brown sugar (or less,
    to taste)
¾ cup applesauce
1 teaspoon Worcestershire sauce
salt, to taste

Preheat oven to 325°F. In a skillet, brown hamburger and onion in the butter.

Place hamburger and onion in a large casserole dish, then stir in remaining ingredients. Bake for 45 minutes.

→DANDELION GREENS←

Pioneers could easily find dandelion greens on the prairies and trails.

> 3 cups dandelion greens, packed
> olive oil, to taste
> apple cider vinegar, to taste
> salt, to taste

In a large bowl, toss the greens with the desired amount of oil, vinegar, and salt.

☞ *Anybody born while the mulberries are ripe has a good chance of being redheaded.*

→PIONEER LETTUCE SALAD←

Lettuce is a cool-weather crop that is mostly resilient to light frosts. It has a long harvest season and made an excellent spring crop for pioneers, who had to survive harsh winters with few fresh vegetables.

> 1 head of fresh lettuce, rinsed
> 1 cup cream
> ¼ cup apple cider vinegar
> 1 teaspoon sugar
> ¼ teaspoon salt
> dash of pepper

In a large bowl, tear or shred the lettuce leaves. In a separate bowl, whisk the remaining ingredients together. Pour the desired amount of dressing on each serving of salad.

⇥COLESLAW⇤

Coleslaw came from the Dutch pioneers, who called it koolsalade, *meaning "cabbage salad."*

> 6 cups shredded cabbage
> 1 cup grated carrots
> ⅓ cup grated onion
> ½ cup milk
> ⅓ cup sour cream
> 2 tablespoons butter
> 3 tablespoons white vinegar
> 2 tablespoons flour
> 2 teaspoons sugar
> 1 teaspoon ground mustard
> 1 teaspoon salt

Put the cabbage, carrots, and onion in a large mixing bowl.

In a saucepan over medium heat, stir together the remaining ingredients. When the dressing is smooth and well blended, remove it from the heat.

Let the dressing cool, then stir the desired amount into the coleslaw.

⇥DUMPLINGS⇤

Dumplings—pieces of steamed or boiled dough—were most popular among pioneers from England and Germany. However, almost every culture in American pioneer history served some form of dumplings with meat, to add bulk to the meal when vegetables were scarce.

> 3 cups milk
> 1½ tablespoons butter
> 1½ cups flour
> ¼ teaspoon salt
> 5 eggs

In a small saucepan, cook the milk, butter, flour, and salt over medium heat, stirring frequently, until it forms a ball. Remove from heat and beat in the eggs.

Cook the dumplings in soup of choice over low heat. Place the batter by the spoonful on top of the hot soup. If you are steaming the dumplings, place a tight-fitting lid on top of the pan and cook for 10 to 12 minutes (make sure you don't lift the lid during this time). If you are boiling the dumplings, leave the lid off, and flip the dumplings over after 5 to 6 minutes.

⇥HUSH PUPPIES⇥

Hush puppies were invented by Southern Native Americans (Cherokee, Choctaw, Creek, and so forth) and shared with Southern settlers. Today, these fried cornmeal balls are commonly served with fried fish.

    cooking oil (peanut, canola, or
        vegetable)
    1 cup cornmeal
    ⅓ cup flour
    ⅓ teaspoon baking soda
    ⅓ teaspoon salt
    ½ cup finely chopped onion
    ¾ cup buttermilk
    1 egg

Fill a large skillet about ⅓ full with oil, then heat the oil over medium heat.

In a mixing bowl, whisk the remaining ingredients together until the batter is smooth. Carefully drop the batter in the hot oil by the teaspoonful.

Hush puppies usually take about 5 minutes to fry, and you will need to flip them over halfway through cooking. Once they are done, remove them from the oil and place them on paper towels to dry.

⇥GRITS⇤

For many centuries before the British colonies were established in America, Native Americans ate a mushy form of boiled corn. The Native Americans shared this dish with the colonists, who called it "grits." It is still a popular breakfast side dish in the South.

    4½ cups water
    1 cup regular grits
    1 teaspoon salt
    2 tablespoons butter
    ¼ cup milk
    pepper, to taste

In a saucepan, bring the water and salt to a boil. Stir in the grits and continue to stir frequently for 30 to 40 minutes, or until the grits have a soft, mushy consistency. Stir in the milk and butter, then add pepper to taste.

→HOMEMADE NOODLES←

The Chinese were the first to make long, thin noodles from flour. In the 13th century, Marco Polo brought noodles to Venice. Homemade noodles are still a treasure in Italy, where almost every neighborhood has a store strictly devoted to making and selling homemade noodles. Early European and Asian immigrants brought their love for noodles— and their techniques for making them—to America. Adding homemade noodles was an inexpensive way for pioneers to bulk up their soups and stews.

    2 cups flour
    2 eggs
    1 teaspoon salt

Place the flour in a mound on the counter and make a well in the center. In a small bowl, beat the eggs and salt together, then pour into the flour well. Using your hands, gradually knead the flour and eggs together until a nice dough is formed. Roll out the dough until thin. Cut the noodles into the desired shape. If you are not using the noodles immediately, lay them on a parchment paper-lined cookie sheet, then freeze them. Once the noodles are frozen, place them in a freezer bag and place them back in the freezer for future use.

☞ *Corn is not ready to grind into meal until it's dry as an old maid's kiss.*

Breads and Biscuits

Grandma's Bustle Oven

My Grandma's bustle oven
Protruded out in back
But it sure baked good muffins,
Bread and gingersnack.

It took three hours to heat it
Each brick must be hot through.
All the children liked to come
They got a taste of something new.

Along the side there always was
A fireplace for cooking food.
The crowds who came to Grandma's
Were always in an eating mood.

Whether it was rainy or shiny
It was the best place to be,
Near Grandma's bustle oven
And the food she served to me.

MARY TAYLOR

→APPLE BRAN BREAD←

Bran is the outer layer of the wheat berry that is cast off during the wheat-grinding process. Most pioneers, when returning from the mill after taking their wheat to be ground, would have both flour and bran to use as cooking staples throughout the year.

1½ cups flour
¼ cup sugar
½ teaspoon salt
½ cup fresh apple chunks (or reconstituted dried apples)
1½ cups wheat bran
1 cup buttermilk
¼ cup molasses
¼ cup applesauce
1 egg
2 tablespoons warm water
1 teaspoon baking soda

Preheat oven to 325°F. Lightly butter a bread pan. Sift the flour, sugar, and salt together. In a large mixing bowl, combine the flour mixture with the apples, bran, buttermilk, molasses, applesauce, and egg. In a separate bowl, stir the warm water and baking soda together, then stir the mixture into the batter. Spread the batter into the prepared bread pan.

Bake for about 45 minutes, or until a toothpick inserted in the middle of the bread comes out clean.

→IRISH SODA BREAD←

Soda bread became popular in Ireland in the 1800s, when yeast was hard to come by. The original recipes contained only flour, buttermilk, baking soda, and salt. Soda bread was served with freshly churned butter.

3½ cups flour
1 teaspoon salt
1 teaspoon baking soda
2 cups buttermilk

Preheat oven to 375°F. Lightly butter a bread pan. In a large mixing bowl, combine all ingredients and knead slightly. Roll the dough into a loaf and place in the prepared pan. Bake for 25 to 30 minutes, or until the crust is golden brown and the inside is no longer sticky.

→OATMEAL BREAD←

In the cool, wet summers of Northwest Europe, oats are much easier to grow than wheat, barley, or rye. Therefore, oats are a staple food in countries like Scotland and Ireland, and they are even grown successfully in Iceland (see http://en.wikipedia.org/wiki/Oat). Because oatmeal bread was a favorite food of early Scottish immigrants, it soon became popular in America.

> 1½ cups milk
> 1 cup rolled oats
> 1 cup raisins
> 1 egg, well beaten
> ¼ cup molasses
> 2 cups flour
> 1½ tablespoons baking powder
> 1 teaspoon salt
> 2 tablespoons butter, melted

Preheat oven to 325ºF. Lightly butter a bread pan. In a small saucepan, heat the milk but don't let it boil. Remove from heat and stir in the oats and raisins. Cool for about 10 minutes, then stir in the egg and molasses.

In a separate bowl, sift together the flour, baking powder, and salt. Gradually stir the sifted mixture into the batter. Stir in the melted butter.

Spread the batter into the prepared bread pan and bake for about an hour, or until a toothpick inserted in the center of the loaf comes out clean.

→WHEAT BREAD←

Wheat was commonly grown by settlers, so wheat bread was a daily staple at the pioneer table.

> 1 cup warm water
> 1½ teaspoons active dry yeast
> ¼ cup honey
> 1⅔ cups bread flour
> 2 tablespoon butter, melted
> ⅓ teaspoon salt
> 1 cup plus 3 tablespoons whole-
>   wheat flour

In a large mixing bowl, stir together the warm water, yeast, and 2 tablespoons honey. Stir in the bread flour, cover with a towel, and let sit for about 30 minutes.

Mix in 1 tablespoon melted butter, 2 tablespoons honey, and salt. Stir in ½ cup whole-wheat flour. Put the dough on a lightly floured surface and gradually knead in the remaining flour. Lightly oil the mixing bowl, place the dough in it, and turn the dough over so that both sides are coated with oil. Cover dough with a dish towel and let rise until it doubles in size (about an hour).

Preheat oven to 350°F. Shape the dough into a loaf and place it in a lightly buttered bread pan. Bake for 25 to 30 minutes, then lightly brush with 1 tablespoon butter.

→BUTTERMILK HONEY BREAD←

This is a traditional soft, white farm bread, perfect for slicing and making into sandwiches.

1 teaspoon active dry yeast
3 cups flour
1½ teaspoons salt
½ teaspoon sugar
1½ tablespoons honey
1 tablespoon butter (soft)
¾ cup lukewarm buttermilk
3 ounces warm water

In a large mixing bowl, combine the buttermilk and water, then stir in the yeast until it is dissolved. Sprinkle the flour over the liquid. Make a well in the center of the flour and place the remaining ingredients in the well. With your hands, knead the mixture until it forms a dough. Cover it with a towel and let rise until it doubles in size (about 1 to 1½ hours).

Lightly coat a bread pan with butter. Knead dough again, then form into a loaf. Place the dough into the prepared pan and cover with a towel. Let rise for 1 more hour, then bake at 375°F for 30 to 35 minutes, or until the bread is golden brown and cooked throughout.

☞ *In the breadbox of your affections, remember me as a crumb.*

⁌MAPLE OATMEAL BREAD⁌

Native Americans were the first to remove sap from maple trees, then boil it down to produce a deliciously sweet syrup that stored well all winter long. The Ojibwa called it sheesheegummavvis, *which means "sap flows fast." Pioneers learned to make maple syrup, and they often added it to baked breads and cakes.*

1⅓ cups water
2 tablespoons 100% maple syrup
1 teaspoon yeast
3¼ cups all-purpose flour
¾ cup whole-wheat flour
½ cup rolled oats
2 tablespoons oat or wheat bran
1 teaspoon salt
1 teaspoon sugar
3 tablespoons soft butter

In a large bowl, stir together the water, maple syrup, and yeast. Let dissolve for about 5 minutes.

Stir in the all-purpose flour, salt, and sugar. Next, knead in the whole-wheat flour, oats, bran, and soft butter. Continue kneading until all of the flour is fully incorporated into the dough.

Take the dough out of the bowl and lightly oil the bottom and sides of the bowl. Return the dough to the bowl, then turn the dough over to oil both sides. Cover the bowl with plastic wrap and let the dough rise for 1½ hours.

Lightly grease a loaf pan. Gently knead the dough on a lightly floured surface and form into a loaf. Place the dough into the prepared loaf pan. Cover with plastic and let dough rise about 45 minutes.

Preheat oven to 350ºF. Bake loaf for 35 to 40 minutes, or until it has turned a golden brown color.

☞ *If you drop a piece of buttered bread upside down on the floor, it will soon rain.*

→BELGIAN MOLASSES BREAD←

Molasses was a very common sweetener before refined sugar became available, and even then many settlers continued to use molasses because it was less expensive than refined sugar. Belgian immigrants brought to America their recipes for molasses bread, of which the recipe below is an example. Eventually, Belgian molasses bread evolved into plain old molasses bread, which tastes only slightly different.

> 1½ teaspoons yeast
> ¾ cup warm milk
> ½ cup plus 1 tablespoon warm water
> 2½ cups all-purpose flour
> 1 teaspoon salt
> ½ cup whole-wheat flour
> 1 tablespoon butter, at room
>   temperature
> 4 tablespoons molasses
> butter

In a large mixing bowl, stir together the yeast, warm milk, and warm water until the yeast is dissolved. Stir in 1 cup all-purpose flour plus the salt, whole-wheat flour, soft butter, and molasses. Gradually knead in the remaining flour.

Lift up the dough, then place a dab of oil in the bowl and spread it around the bottom and sides of the bowl. Place the bread back in the bowl and turn the dough over to oil both sides. Cover the bowl with plastic and let the dough rise for 1 hour, or until it doubles in size.

Knead the dough slightly, then turn it out onto a floured surface. Roll out the dough into a rectangle. Gather up a long edge of the dough and curl it up, rolling it back onto the dough to make a log. Tuck the ends under the loaf and place the loaf into a greased bread-loaf pan. Cover with plastic and let rise another 45 minutes to 1 hour (it should double in size again).

Preheat oven to 350°F. Bake bread for 35 to 40 minutes, or until the crust is a lovely brown color. After you remove the bread from the oven, lightly brush the top of the loaf with butter.

☞ *Slow as molasses, warm as toast.*

⁺POTATO BREAD⁺

In the 1800s, potato bread became popular in Ireland as a way to use leftover mashed potatoes. It is a light and airy bread with a slight yellow color. In Ireland, potato bread is known by various regional names, such as fadge, slims, potato cake, potato farls, and tatie bread (see wikipedia.org/wiki/Potato_bread). Irish immigrants brought their potato bread to America, where it gradually became popular.

¾ cup potato water (explained
    below)

¼ cup milk

2 tablespoons butter

1½ teaspoons salt

2 tablespoons sugar

¾ cup plus 1 tablespoon mashed
    potato

3 cups plus 2 tablespoons bread
    flour

1½ teaspoons rapid-rising yeast

Peel and boil 1 or 2 potatoes in water. When the potatoes are soft, save ¾ cup of the potato water and mash the potato without adding any milk, butter, or salt.

In a small saucepan, stir together the potato water, milk, and butter. Heat over medium heat just until the butter is melted. Pour into a large mixing bowl. Beat in the salt, sugar, and mashed potato. Add about half of the flour, combining well.

When the dough has cooled slightly, sprinkle the yeast over the dough, then beat the dough until the yeast is incorporated throughout. Add the rest of the flour and knead until a soft dough forms (you may need to add a bit more flour if the dough is too sticky). Knead for a few minutes.

Take the dough out of the bowl, lightly oil the bowl, then place the dough back in the bowl and turn the dough over to coat both sides with oil. Cover with a towel and let rise about 45 minutes.

Turn the dough onto a lightly floured surface and punch it down, then form it into a loaf. Place in a lightly greased bread pan. Cover with a towel and let rise another 40 minutes.

Preheat oven to 375°F. Bake the bread for 30 to 35 minutes. It is done when it is golden brown on top and makes a hollow sound if you tap the bottom of the pan.

⟶RYE BREAD⟵

Rye bread is common in many areas of the world. This particular kind of homemade rye bread was a favorite among the German immigrants and pioneers.

1 package active dry yeast
¼ cup warm water
¾ cup warm milk
1 tablespoon sugar
½ teaspoon salt
¼ cup molasses
1 tablespoon butter, at room
    temperature
1½ cups plus 2 tablespoons rye flour
¾ cup bread flour

In a small bowl, stir the yeast into the warm water.

In a large mixing bowl, beat the milk, sugar, and salt. Beat in the yeast mixture, molasses, butter, and ½ cup rye flour. Using a wooden spoon, gradually stir in the remaining rye and bread flours until the dough is stiff enough to use your hands to knead.

Knead for about 5 minutes, adding a little more flour if the dough is too sticky. Cover dough with a towel and let rise until it doubles in size (about an hour).

Punch down the dough and form into a loaf shape. Place on a lightly buttered or parchment paper-lined cookie sheet, then cover it again and let it rise for another hour.

Preheat oven to 375°F. Bake the bread on the cookie sheet for about 30 minutes, or until the crust is golden brown.

☞ *Plant pumpkin seeds in May,*
and they will run away.
Plant pumpkin seeds in June,
and they will come too soon.

→HERB BREAD←

This recipe was adapted from Recipes Old & New, Tried & True, from The City Beautiful, Nauvoo *(Nauvoo Restoration, Inc., 1994).*

> 1 cup water
> 1 cup milk
> ¼ cup vegetable oil
> 1½ cups whole-wheat flour
> ¼ cup sugar
> 1 tablespoon onion pulp
> 1½ teaspoons garlic salt
> ½ teaspoon dried basil flakes
> ½ teaspoon dried oregano flakes
> ½ teaspoon dried parsley flakes
> 2 packages yeast
> 1 egg
> 2½ cups all-purpose flour

Heat the water, milk, and oil in a saucepan until just warm, then pour the mixture into a large bowl. Stir in the remaining ingredients, mixing well. Place the dough in a buttered 2-quart casserole dish. Cover and let rise about 1 hour. Preheat the oven to 350°F. Bake bread for about 45 minutes. Lightly butter the top of the bread after removing it from the oven.

→PUMPKIN BREAD←

Pumpkins were a pioneer staple in wintertime, when fruits and vegetables were hard to come by. If left whole and kept in a cool, dry place such as a cellar, pumpkins could potentially last all winter, making them a vital source of nutrition.

> 2 cups boiled and mashed pumpkin
> 1 cup sugar
> 1 cup brown sugar
> ½ cup vegetable oil
> 1 egg
> 2½ cups flour
> ½ teaspoon salt
> ½ teaspoon ground cinnamon
> ½ teaspoon ground cloves
> ¼ teaspoon ground nutmeg
> 2 teaspoons baking soda
> 1 cup raisins or chopped walnuts (or
>   a mixture of both)

Preheat oven to 350°F. Lightly butter the bottom and sides of a bread pan. In a large mixing bowl, whisk together the pumpkin, sugars, oil, and egg. Gradually stir in the remaining ingredients, leaving the nuts and raisins for last.

Spread the batter into the prepared bread pan and bake for about an hour, or until a toothpick inserted in the center of the loaf comes out clean.

→PUMPERNICKEL BREAD←

Pumpernickel bread originated in 15th-century Germany. To give it a rich, dark color, the bread was baked at very low temperatures for 16 to 24 hours. After pumpernickel bread was brought to North America, the recipe was altered. Baking times were shortened, the oven temperature was raised, and ingredients such as cocoa powder, molasses, and coffee were added to give the bread a deep brown color.

> 1¼ cups warm water
> 2¼ teaspoons yeast
> ⅓ cup molasses
> 2 cups whole-wheat flour
> 1½ cups rye flour
> 1 teaspoon salt
> 2 tablespoons vegetable oil
> 2 tablespoons cocoa powder
> 1 tablespoon caraway seeds

Stir the warm water, yeast, and molasses in a small bowl and set aside until the top is foamy (5 to 10 minutes).

In a large mixing bowl, stir together the remaining ingredients. Add the yeast mixture. Knead with your hands until everything is well combined and a dough is formed.

Lift the dough and place a dab of oil in the bowl. Using your fingers, spread the oil on the bottom and sides of the bowl. Place the dough back in the bowl, then turn the dough over to oil both sides. Cover with plastic wrap and let rise for 1 hour.

Punch the dough down, then form into a round loaf. Place on a baking sheet. Cover and let rise another hour.

Preheat oven to 350ºF. Bake the loaf for 40 to 50 minutes.

☞ *To make good bread, let it rise with the sun.*

→SOURDOUGH BREAD←

Sourdough bread was a staple in Northern California during the gold rush, and it is still very popular there today. In fact, some long-standing bakeries can trace their sourdough starters back to California's territorial period.

Starter

    1 teaspoon yeast
    1 cup warm water
    1 cup flour

In a large jar, mix the yeast and water together, then stir in the flour. Loosely cover the jar and place in a warm place for 4 to 8 days to ferment. When the mixture is foamy and has a pleasant sour smell, it is ready. Keep the starter covered in the refrigerator until ready to use.

When you remove some starter for bread making, replace it by adding equal amounts of flour and water to the jar. (If you take out 1 cup of starter, put in 1 cup water and 1 cup flour.) Then add a small pinch of sugar. Allow starter to sit out until bubbly again, then return it to the refrigerator. If a brown liquid forms on the top of the starter, just stir the liquid back in. (The brown liquid is alcohol that was produced during fermentation; it will cook out when the bread is baked.) If your starter turns pink or orange, throw it away and start over.

Bread

    2 cups flour
    1½ cups sourdough starter
    ¾ teaspoon salt
    1 tablespoon cornmeal

In a large bowl, mix together the flour, starter, and salt. Knead until a dough is formed. Remove the dough and lightly oil the bottom and sides of the bowl. Return the dough to the bowl, then turn the dough over to oil both sides. Cover the bowl with plastic wrap and let dough rise for 1 to 1½ hours.

Turn dough onto a floured surface and gently knead out the bubbles. Form into a round loaf, pinching any ends underneath. Place dough on a well-floured surface, then cover with a towel and let rise for another hour.

Preheat oven to 400°F. Place a cooking stone on the bottom rack in the oven to preheat.

Using a sharp knife, cut a large *X* into the top of the round loaf. Lightly dust the bottom of the loaf with cornmeal, then place on the heated stone (or a heavy baking sheet).

Bake for about 1 hour, or until the crust is golden brown and a hollow sound is made when you thump the bottom of the loaf.

⇥SALT-RISING BREAD⇤

This dense white bread was made by pioneers when yeast was unavailable. According to Wikipedia.org, salt-rising bread was popular in Scotland and Ireland in the 17th century, and the tradition is kept alive in areas of the midwestern and eastern United States. The bread has a cheesy flavor due to its unique fermentation process.

1 cup milk
1 tablespoon sugar
7 tablespoons white cornmeal
1 teaspoon salt
2 cups lukewarm water
3 tablespoons shortening
2 tablespoons sugar
10½ cups all-purpose flour, divided

Scald milk and stir in sugar, cornmeal, and salt. Place in jar and cover with cheesecloth. Set jar in water as hot as the hand can stand. Allow to sit for 6 to 7 hours in a warm place, about 115°F; the mixture has fermented enough when gas can be heard escaping.

Add water, shortening, sugar, and 2 cups flour; beat well. Put in a container, then place the container in a pan of water. Maintain heat at 115°F until the mixture is very light and full of bubbles.

When ready to make bread, add about 8½ cups flour to the mixture. Knead for 10 minutes. Mold into 4 loaves and put in greased 5 x 9-inch loaf pans. Cover and let rise until dough is 2½ times the original size.

Bake loaves at 375°F for 10 minutes. Lower temperature to 350°F and bake for 25 minutes longer, or until the bread turns a light golden brown color.

☞ *He who hesitates is lost.*

⊹SPOON BREAD⊹

Spoon bread is a pudding-like bread that is usually eaten with a spoon or fork. In his book Southern Food, *John Egerton says that spoon bread probably originated in Virginia around 1824. However, some historians claim that spoon bread can be traced back to a Native American porridge called* suppawn *or* suppone.

> 3 eggs, separated
> ¾ cup flour
> 1 teaspoon salt
> 1½ teaspoons baking powder
> ¾ teaspoon baking soda
> ¾ cup cornmeal
> 1 cup boiling water
> 3 teaspoons butter
> 1 cup buttermilk

Beat egg whites until stiff. In a separate bowl, sift dry ingredients except cornmeal. In a large mixing bowl, slowly pour boiling water over cornmeal; stir until cool.

Add butter, egg yolks, and flour mixture alternately with buttermilk to cornmeal mush. Beat well, then fold in egg whites.

Spread dough in an 8-inch square glass baking dish, or a 1½-quart casserole dish. Bake at 350°F for about 30 to 35 minutes, or until the spoon bread is set and lightly browned. Serve hot with plenty of butter.

⊹CHALLAH⊹

Challah is a beautiful braided bread brought to North America by Jewish immigrants. Traditionally, the bread was made to celebrate holy days and Sabbath days. These large loaves, called double loaves, symbolize the manna sent from heaven to feed the ancient Israelites as they wandered in the wilderness after their escape from Egypt. Manna did not fall on the Sabbath, so the Israelites were commanded to gather enough manna for two days on the day before each Sabbath. The tradition of the double loaf stems from this ancient practice.

Dough

> 1 cup warm water
> 1 cup warm milk
> 1 packages yeast (4½ teaspoons)

6 to 7 cups flour
½ cup sugar
1 teaspoon salt
¼ cup butter, melted
1 egg

Topping

1 egg
1 tablespoon water
1 tablespoon sesame seeds or poppy
    seeds (optional)

In a large mixing bowl, dissolve the yeast in the warm water and milk. Stir in the sugar and salt. Add 3 cups of flour, along with the melted butter and the egg. Mix well, then mix in 3 additional cups of flour. Knead until the ingredients are thoroughly combined and a dough is formed.

Remove the dough from the bowl and place a dab of oil on the bottom and sides of the bowl. Return the dough to the bowl, then turn the dough over to oil both sides. Cover bowl with a damp towel and let dough rise until the it doubles in size (about 1 hour).

Place the dough on a floured surface and press gently to deflate. With a sharp knife, cut the dough into three equal pieces. Work with one piece of dough at a time, keeping the other pieces lightly covered in plastic wrap so that they do not dry out.

Using your hands, roll each piece of dough into a long rope (20+ inches long), putting flour on your hands as needed to prevent sticking. Place the three long ropes side by side and pinch the tops together. Starting at the top, braid the far right rope over the middle one, then braid the far left rope over the middle. Alternate until you get to the end. Pinch the bottom of the dough pieces together and tuck them under the braid.

Move the braided dough to a greased baking sheet, then cover with plastic wrap. Set the dough in a warm spot and let rise another 30 to 45 minutes, or until it doubles in size again.

Preheat oven to 375°F. For the topping, whisk together the egg and water, then brush the mixture over the braid. If using sesame or poppy seeds, sprinkle them evenly over the braid. Bake loaf for about 35 to 45 minutes, or until the crust is brown.

→JOHNNY CAKES←

Johnny cakes are cornmeal flatbreads that were a staple among early Americans. Native Americans used ground corn for cooking, and they made these little cakes long before European settlers arrived. Now johnny cakes are a specialty of New Englanders.

2 cups cornmeal
1½ teaspoons salt
1 tablespoon honey
2½ cups boiling water

Heat a griddle or large frying pan over medium heat, then lightly coat with butter or oil. In a mixing bowl, stir together the cornmeal, salt, and honey. Gradually stir in the water until a batter is formed (all of the water may not be needed).

For each cake, drop about ¼ cup of batter onto the heated surface. Cook for about 5 minutes, flipping after about 2½ minutes.

☞ *For sweetness honey, for love, a wife.*

→SOURDOUGH PANCAKES←

Sourdough evolved because pioneer cooks lacked the usual sources of yeast and leavening. When they traveled, they would simply carry a little sourdough starter with them for the next batch of bread. Making pancakes was a good way to use any extra sourdough starter. These pancakes are so light that they almost melt in your mouth.

2 cups sourdough starter (see
   sourdough bread recipe, page
   110), room temperature
2 tablespoons granulated sugar
1 egg
4 tablespoons vegetable oil
½ teaspoon salt
1 teaspoon baking soda
1 tablespoon warm water

The night before you plan to make the pancakes, remove the sourdough starter from the refrigerator so it can come to room temperature.

In a large bowl, mix the sourdough starter with the sugar, egg, oil, and salt. Set aside.

In a small bowl, dilute 1 teaspoon baking soda in 1 tablespoon warm water.

When ready to cook pancakes, gently fold the baking soda–water mixture into the prepared pancake batter; do not beat. (Do not add baking soda–water mixture to the pancake batter until you are ready to cook the pancakes.) Let the mixture bubble and foam for 1 to 2 minutes.

Heat an oiled griddle. For each pancake, pour ¼ to ½ cup batter on the hot griddle. Cook for 1 to 2 minutes on each side or until golden brown. Serve pancakes hot.

→BUCKWHEAT PANCAKES←

Buckwheat was a staple among most pioneers, particularly those from Eastern Europe. A pseudocereal, buckwheat comes from an Asian plant that is not at all related to wheat. The starchy seeds of the buckwheat plant are used for animal fodder or ground into buckwheat flour.

    1 cup buckwheat flour
    ¾ cup whole-wheat flour

1 tablespoon sugar
2 teaspoons baking powder
1 teaspoon salt
2 eggs
⅓ cup butter, softened
1⅔ cup milk

Heat a large skillet or griddle to medium, then lightly coat with butter. In a mixing bowl, whisk all ingredients together until a smooth batter is formed. Drop about ⅓ cup batter per pancake onto the heated surface. Cook until the batter forms bubbles on top (about 3 minutes), then flip over and cook another 3 to 4 minutes.

☞ *Half past cornbread and goin' on biscuits.*

→FLAPJACKS←

A flapjack is a small, thick pancake that was a popular food among pioneers. Flapjacks were easy to make and could be eaten with homemade jam, maple syrup, or honey, or wrapped around a piece of meat to form a sandwich. Traditionally, flapjacks are served in a stack with syrup and butter. Bacon or sausage often rounds out the meal.

> 1½ cups flour
> 2 teaspoons baking powder
> 1 tablespoon sugar
> 2 tablespoons butter, melted
> 1 teaspoon salt
> 1 egg
> 1¼ cup milk
> oil or butter for frying

Mix all ingredients together. Batter should be about the same consistency as regular pancake batter.

Cook on a well-oiled griddle over medium heat. Flip pancakes when bubbles form on top. Serve hot.

→CORNBREAD←

Cornbread is one of the oldest foods on the American continents. Native Americans would dry corn, grind it into powder, and make a simple cornbread that was dense and traveled easily. While Native Americans baked small cornbread cakes in clay ovens, pioneers baked the cakes in cast-iron pots.

> 2 eggs
> 2 cups milk
> ¼ cup vegetable oil
> 2 cups cornmeal
> 2 cups flour
> 2 teaspoons baking powder
> 2 teaspoons salt

Preheat oven to 325°F. Lightly butter a 9-inch square baking dish. In a mixing bowl, beat together the eggs, milk, and oil. In a separate bowl, whisk together the remaining ingredients, then gradually stir them into the wet mixture.

Bake for 45 to 50 minutes, or until a toothpick inserted in the middle of the cornbread comes out clean.

→SWEET POTATO BISCUITS←

The origin of the sweet potato biscuit is unknown, but it probably came with the advent of baking powder in the 1800s, as well as the large-scale commercial growing of sweet potatoes on Virginia's eastern shore in the late 1800s. Pillsbury's 1914 cookbook included a sweet potato biscuit recipe that calls for baking soda and buttermilk. In the South, these flaky biscuits were known as "Sunday-morning biscuits" because biscuits were often eaten on Sundays before families went to church.

1 medium sweet potato
½ cup (1 stick) butter, melted
¼ cup brown sugar, firmly packed
2¼ cups all-purpose flour
1 tablespoon baking powder
¾ teaspoon salt
½ teaspoon baking soda
¼ teaspoon ground cinnamon
⅔ cup buttermilk

Preheat oven to 375°F. Pierce sweet potato with a fork in several places. Bake potato until tender, approximately 1 hour. Remove from oven.

Cut sweet potato in half and cool slightly. Scoop potato flesh into a small bowl and cool completely.

Place 1 cup sweet potato flesh in a large bowl. Add butter and brown sugar; beat until smooth.

Sift flour, baking powder, salt, baking soda, and cinnamon into a medium bowl. Mix dry ingredients with sweet potato alternately with buttermilk in 3 additions, beginning and ending with dry ingredients.

Transfer dough to a generously floured surface. Roll out dough until it is ¾ inch thick. Using a 2-inch round cookie cutter, cut out biscuits. Place on an ungreased baking sheet.

Bake biscuits until golden and puffy, approximately 20 to 25 minutes. Transfer baking sheet to rack and cool slightly. Serve biscuits warm or at room temperature.

☞ *Turnabout is fair play.*

→BUTTERMILK BISCUITS←

Buttermilk is the liquid that is left over from churning butter. The liquid absorbs airborne bacteria, which sours and thickens the liquid. Buttermilk was used for many things in the pioneer kitchen, including the ever-popular buttermilk biscuits.

> 2 cups flour
> 1 teaspoon salt
> 1 teaspoon baking powder
> ½ teaspoon baking soda
> ¼ cup butter
> ¾ cup buttermilk

Preheat oven to 425°F. In a large mixing bowl, sift together the flour, salt, baking powder, and baking soda. Cut the butter into the mixture with 2 butter knives or a pastry blender. Stir the buttermilk into the dough and form into a large ball.

Place the ball on a lightly floured surface and roll out with a floured rolling pin. Cut into circles with a 2-inch biscuit cutter or the brim of an upside-down drinking glass.

Put the dough circles on an ungreased cookie sheet, then bake for about 15 minutes or until the biscuits are light golden brown.

→MORMON SODA BISCUITS←

Among the largest pioneer movements to the western United States were the "Mormons," or members of The Church of Jesus Christ of Latter-Day Saints, who settled the territory of Utah and the surrounding regions. These soda biscuits were popular among the Mormon pioneers.

> 3 cups flour
> 1 teaspoon salt
> 1 teaspoon sugar
> 1 teaspoon baking soda
> 3 tablespoons butter or shortening
> 2 cups buttermilk

Preheat oven to 425°F. Line a cookie sheet with parchment paper. In a large mixing bowl, sift together the flour, salt, sugar, and baking soda. Cut in the butter or shortening using 2 butter knives or a pastry blender. Slowly stir in the buttermilk until a soft dough is formed.

Roll out dough on a lightly floured surface, then cut into circles. Place the circles on the prepared cookie sheet in rows about 2 inches apart. Bake for about 15 minutes or until the biscuits are light golden brown.

⇾MILK BISCUITS⇽

"In the Virginia of the olden time no breakfast or tea table was thought to be properly furnished without a plate of . . . biscuits" (Virginia Cookery Book *[1885]).*

    2 cups flour
    3 tablespoons sugar
    1 tablespoon baking powder
    ¾ teaspoon salt
    6 tablespoons butter, cut into small
        chunks
    1 cup milk

Preheat oven to 400°F. In a mixing bowl, whisk together the flour, sugar, baking powder, and salt. Using a pastry blender or two butter knives, cut the butter into the flour mixture until the pieces of butter are about the size of small peas. With a large wooden spoon, stir in the milk.

On a lightly floured surface, use a lightly floured rolling pin to roll out the dough until it is about ⅓ inch thick. Use a 2-inch biscuit cutter (or the brim of a glass) to cut the biscuits out of the dough. Take the scraps and roll them out again, then cut them and continue until all of the dough has been cut into round pieces. Place pieces on a cooking stone or cookie sheet about an inch apart. Bake biscuits about 15 minutes, then cool on a wire rack.

☞ *Better the guests wait on the biscuits than the biscuits wait on the guests.*

→SCONES←

Our scone-making immigrant ancestors hailed from England, Scotland, and Ireland. The original scones, before they ever made it the America, were made with oats and shaped in a large, round dough circle that was cut into 4 or 6 wedges and cooked on a griddle over an open fire. This type of scone is commonly served hot with butter and honey.

> 1½ cups flour
> 1½ teaspoons baking powder
> ½ teaspoon baking soda
> ½ teaspoon salt
> 3 tablespoons butter
> ½ cup buttermilk

Preheat oven to 450°F. In a large mixing bowl, sift together the flour, baking powder, baking soda, and salt. Cut the butter into the flour mixture with 2 butter knives or a pastry blender. Stir in the buttermilk until a soft dough is formed.

Knead the dough on a lightly floured surface for about 1 minute. Divide the dough into 2 balls, then roll out each ball until it is about ½ inch thick.

Place the rounds on an ungreased baking sheet and cut each round into 6 wedges. Pull the wedges out so they are about 1 inch apart. Bake for 10 to 12 minutes.

→POPOVERS←

A derivative of Yorkshire pudding, popovers were originally made with drippings from roast beef or pork. Popovers were brought to America by British immigrants, and in the 1800s the pastries' popularity spread west from New England. These popovers are delicious served with butter and jam.

> 4 eggs
> 1¼ cups milk
> 3 tablespoons butter, melted and
>   slightly cooled
> 1 cup flour
> ¾ teaspoon salt

Preheat oven to 425°F. Heavily butter 12 cups of a muffin pan. Place the eggs, milk, and butter in a blender. Blend on medium speed for about 10 seconds.

Turn off the blender, then add the flour and salt. Blend for another 15 seconds on medium speed.

Pour the batter into the prepared muffin cups until they are about ¾ full. Bake for 25 to 30 minutes, or until the popovers are very puffy and brown. (Do not open the oven door while cooking the popovers, or they may not rise properly.)

Immediately after removing the pan from the oven, tip the pan over a clean kitchen counter until the popovers fall out. Pierce each popover with a thin wooden skewer to allow the steam to escape. Serve immediately.

BAGELS

Jewish Polish immigrants brought their "beygels" to America. Since the 1880s, bagel bakeries have been thriving in New York City, and their popularity soon spread throughout the country. Bagels were originally sold on the streets by individual vendors, who would thread the bagels on long wooden rods to carry and display them.

1 cup warm water
2¼ teaspoons yeast
2 tablespoons sugar, divided
3 cups flour, divided
1 teaspoon salt
1 teaspoon vegetable oil

In a large mixing bowl, stir together the warm water, yeast, and 1½ tablespoons sugar until the yeast and sugar dissolve. Let mixture sit for about 5 minutes (it should be foamy).

Stir in the salt and 2 cups flour. Gradually add the remaining flour as you knead the dough. (This dough will be very thick.)

Lift the dough and place the oil in the bowl, then use your fingers to spread the oil on the bottom and sides of the bowl. Return the dough to the bowl and turn the dough over to oil both sides. Cover bowl with plastic and let dough rise for about 1 hour.

Divide the dough into 6 equal pieces, then form each piece of dough into a ball. Roll each ball into a 4- to 6-inch log. Pinch the ends together. Then put your fingers in the hole and press the ends of the circle on a lightly floured surface as you roll that part as well, fully meshing the ends together so the dough forms a smooth ring. Place the bagels on a large, greased baking sheet and cover with a cloth. Let rise for 30 minutes.

Preheat oven to 400°F. Add ½ tablespoon sugar to a pot of water, then bring the water to a boil. Gently lower the bagels into the boiling water in batches. Boil each bagel for 30 seconds to 1 minute, turning often.

Remove the bagels from the water and place them on another greased cookie sheet. Bake for 5 minutes, then turn bagels over and bake for another 30 to 35 minutes.

→CORN TORTILLAS←

Tortillas are known as the "bread of Mexico" and originated many centuries ago with the Aztecs of central America. Women would put a few handfuls of soaked corn kernels on a flat surface and use a stoneroller to scrub them back and forth. This process created the masa that was used to make corn tortillas.

2 cups masa harina
1½ cups water

Mash ingredients together in a mixing bowl. Take small clumps of the dough and flatten them out with your hands, a rolling pin, or a tortilla press. Place each piece of dough on a hot griddle and cook for 45 seconds to 1 minute on each side.

→FLOUR TORTILLAS←

In Spanish, the word tortilla *means "little cake." The tortilla is a staple in both old-time and modern Mexican cuisine.*

2 cups flour
1½ teaspoons baking powder
1 teaspoon salt
2 teaspoons vegetable oil
¾ cup warm milk

In a mixing bowl, stir together the flour, baking soda, salt, and oil. Slowly stir in the milk. Knead ingredients together until a soft, sticky ball is formed. Cover dough with a damp towel and let rest for 20 minutes.

Divide the dough into 8 sections, then cover with the damp cloth (don't let sections touch) and let rest another 10 minutes.

On a lightly floured surface, roll out the tortillas. Cook them on a hot griddle or frying pan for about 30 seconds on each side.

→NAVAJO FRY BREAD←

The story of Navajo fry bread is a very sad one. In the mid-1800s, the Navajo were captured and sent on a 300-mile "long walk" that led to a camp they would share with the Mescalero Apache. The Navajos that didn't starve to death on the walk survived on extremely meager (and often rancid) government rations. The rations of lard, flour, salt, sugar, baking powder, and powdered milk were made into this simple fry bread, which is now a staple food for many Native American tribes.

2 cups flour
1 teaspoon salt
2 teaspoons powdered milk
2 teaspoons baking powder
1 cup water
vegetable oil

Pour oil into a large skillet until it is about 1 inch deep. Turn burner to medium heat.

In a large mixing bowl, sift together the flour, salt, powdered milk, and baking powder. Pour the water over the flour mixture and stir together with a fork (do not knead). With your hands, form the dough into 4 mounds that are well floured on the outside and very sticky on the inside.

Place each piece of dough, 1 or 2 at a time, in the hot oil and let fry on each side for about 3 to 4 minutes.

☞ *Bread dough turns sad (soggy) if it sits too long.*

→SOPAIPILLAS←

Sopaipillas, or fried flat bread, probably originated in Albuquerque, New Mexico, in the 1800s. They are also known as New Mexican quick bread. In most parts of the country, sopaipillas are served as a dessert, but in New Mexico they are served as a savory part of a meal. To serve these sopaipillas as a dessert, sprinkle them with cinnamon sugar immediately after removing them from the oil, then top them with honey, chocolate syrup, and/or whipped cream.

    2 cups flour
    1 teaspoon baking powder
    ½ teaspoon salt
    2 tablespoons soft butter
    ¾ cup warm water
    oil for frying

In a large mixing bowl, stir together the flour, baking powder, salt, and soft butter. Stir in the water, then knead the dough until all of the flour is incorporated. Cover dough and let rise for 20 minutes.

On a floured surface, roll out the dough into a large square about ¼ inch thick. Cut the dough into 3-inch squares.

Fill a large skillet about ½ inch deep with cooking oil, then heat to medium high. Carefully drop the dough pieces into the hot oil and fry on each side for 1 to 2 minutes, or until both sides are golden brown. Drain on paper towels.

☞ *He who has butter on his bread should not stand in the sun.*

YIDDISH PROVERB

Desserts

Home Again

Home again, home again, from a foreign shore,
And oh! It fills my soul with joy
To meet with friends once more.
Here I dropped the parting tear
To cross the ocean's foam,
But now I'm once again with those
Who fondly greet me home.

Sweet music, music soft, lingers 'round the place,
And oh, I feel the childhood charm
That time cannot efface.
Then give me but my homestead roof,
I'll ask no palace dome, for I can live a happy life
With those I love at home.

⇥OATMEAL CAKE⇤

Oats were common in frontier settlements because they were fed to livestock. When rolled or ground, oats could be used to make porridge or cake, among other tasty concoctions.

Cake

- 1¼ cup water
- 1 cup rolled oats
- ½ cup butter, at room temperature
- 1 cup brown sugar
- ½ cup molasses
- 2 eggs, well beaten
- 1 teaspoon ground cinnamon
- 1 tablespoon baking soda
- 1¼ cups flour

Topping

- ⅓ cup butter
- ½ cup brown sugar
- ¼ cup milk
- 1 cup chopped pecans

Preheat oven to 350ºF. Grease a 9 x 13-inch baking dish.

In a saucepan over medium heat, bring the water to a boil. Stir in the oats, turn off the heat, and let stand in the pan (still on the burner) for about 15 minutes.

In a large mixing bowl, cream together the brown sugar, molasses, eggs, and ½ cup butter. Sift the cinnamon, baking soda, and flour into the batter. Stir in the oats.

Spread the batter into the prepared baking pan. Bake for 35 to 40 minutes, or until a toothpick inserted in the center of the cake comes out clean.

After the cake has cooled, melt ⅓ cup butter. Stir in the remaining topping ingredients until the sugar is dissolved. Spread topping over the cake.

☞ *A half-truth is a whole lie.*

YIDDISH PROVERB

⇢HONEY CAKE⇠

Honey cake is a traditional treat for Jewish holidays, particularly Rosh Hashanah, the Jewish New Year.

1 cup honey
½ cup vegetable oil
1 egg
½ cup buttermilk
½ teaspoon salt
1 teaspoon baking soda
½ teaspoon ground cinnamon
2 cups flour

Preheat oven to 375°F. Grease and flour a bundt pan. In a large mixing bowl, whisk together the honey, oil, egg, and buttermilk.

In a separate bowl, whisk together the dry ingredients. Slowly stir the dry mixture into the wet mixture.

Bake the cake for 45 to 55 minutes, or until a toothpick inserted in the center comes out clean. Allow the cake to rest for at least one day before serving.

⇢APPLESAUCE WEDDING CAKE⇠

When a pioneer woman was to be married on the trails or in a new settlement, she would ask each of her friends to bring a cake to the celebration. Her mother would spread applesauce on top of each cake and stack them one atop the other, making a layered cake. It was easy to tell a popular bride by the height of her wedding cake.

Applesauce

5 apples, cored, peeled, and chopped
1 cup water
¼ cup sugar
¼ teaspoon ground cinnamon

Combine all ingredients in a pan. Cover and cook over medium heat for 10 to 15 minutes, or until the apples are soft. Mash the apples with a potato masher or fork.

This applesauce may be used with almost any type of cake, but the varieties most frequently served at pioneer weddings were oatmeal cake (see page 127) and spice cake (see page 133).

→APPLE CAKE←

This type of epplekaka *comes to us from Swedish pioneers.*

Cake

3/4 cup sugar

3/4 cup brown sugar

2 1/4 cups flour

1/4 teaspoon salt

2 teaspoons baking soda

2 teaspoons cinnamon

1/2 cup (1 stick) butter, at room temperature

2 eggs, well beaten

1 cup buttermilk

2 large apples, cored and thinly sliced

Topping

1/2 cup chopped walnuts

1/4 cup brown sugar

1/4 cup sugar

1/2 teaspoon ground cinnamon

Preheat oven to 350°F. Grease and flour a 9 x 13-inch baking dish and set aside.

In a large mixing bowl, stir all of the dry cake ingredients together. In a separate bowl, whisk together all of the wet cake ingredients. Gradually stir the wet mixture into the dry mixture. Stir until the batter is smooth, then gently fold in the apple slices.

Pour the batter into the prepared baking dish. In a small bowl, stir together the topping ingredients, then sprinkle the mixture over the cake batter. Bake for about 45 minutes, or until a toothpick inserted in the center of the cake comes out clean.

☞ *Believe nothing of what you hear, and only half of what you see.*

→GRANDMA CHECKETTS' CHERRY CAKE←

My neighbor Sue Larson provided this recipe, which has been passed down in her family. When Sue's grandma Checketts made the cake, she would use an old china cup with the handle broken off to measure the flour, and she would measure the cake's other dry ingredients in her palm. Sue gives her aunt Nancy the credit for converting the recipe to exact measurements so it could be easily reproduced.

    1 quart bottled Bing cherries, pitted
       and drained
    ¾ cup butter
    1 cup sugar
    3 eggs
    1 teaspoon ground nutmeg
    1 teaspoon ground cloves
    1 cup buttermilk
    2½ cups flour
    1 teaspoon baking soda

Preheat oven to 350ºF. Grease and flour a 9 x 13-inch baking pan. In a large mixing bowl, cream together the butter and sugar until fluffy. Beat in the eggs one at a time. Stir in the nutmeg and cloves, then the flour. Mix well. Gently stir in the cherries.

Pour the batter into the prepared pan and bake for 40 to 50 minutes, or until a toothpick inserted in the center of the cake comes out clean. Top cake with white frosting of choice.

→POUND CAKE←

The pound cake recipe from 18th-century England got its name from the ingredients: 1 pound butter, 1 pound sugar, 1 pound eggs, and 1 pound flour. The simple recipe was perfect for the many thousands of people who could not read, because they could easily memorize the ingredients.

    3 eggs
    1 cup (2 sticks) butter, at room
       temperature
    1 cup sugar
    2 cups flour
    1½ teaspoons vanilla
    ¼ teaspoon salt
    ¼ teaspoon ground nutmeg

Preheat oven to 325°F. Grease the bottom and sides of a bread pan.

In a large mixing bowl, cream together the eggs, butter, and sugar. In half-cup increments, stir in the flour. Stir in the vanilla, salt, and nutmeg.

Spread the batter into the prepared pan and bake for 60 to 65 minutes, or until a toothpick inserted in the center of the cake comes out clean.

✦BABOVKA✦

Babovka is a Czechoslovakian Easter bread that is sweet and that is very close to pound cake or coffee cake. It is often served with tea.

1 cup plus 2 tablespoons warm milk
1 teaspoon yeast
3 cups flour
½ teaspoon salt
5 tablespoons brown sugar
2 egg yolks
5 tablespoons butter
½ cup raisins

Dissolve the yeast in the warm milk, then add 1 cup flour. Let this mixture rise for about 30 minutes (it will be spongy).

Preheat oven to 350°F. Grease or butter a 9-inch tube pan or bundt pan.

Sift the salt with the remaining 2 cups flour; set aside.

In a separate bowl, cream together the brown sugar and butter. Add the flour mixture and stir until well combined. Gradually stir in the yeast mixture, then the raisins.

Spread the dough into the prepared pan and bake for 45 to 50 minutes. The bread is done when a toothpick inserted in the center comes out clean.

☞ *A bellowing cow soon forgets her calf.*

✢STOLLEN✢

Dating back to 15ᵗʰ-century Germany, stollen *is a moist, bread-like fruit cake covered with a sugary topping. The Dutch have a very similar cake called* kerststol.

Fruit

    1 cup fresh cherries, pitted and
        diced (or dried apple chunks, or a
        mixture)
    1 cup raisins
    3 tablespoons orange juice

Sponge

    2 teaspoons yeast
    ¼ cup warm water
    ⅔ cup milk
    1 teaspoon honey
    1 cup flour

Dough

    ⅓ cup honey
    1 egg, well beaten
    ½ cup butter, at room temperature
    1 tablespoon grated lemon zest
    1 teaspoon salt
    ½ teaspoon ground mace
    ½ cup chopped almonds, toasted
    3½ cups flour
    oil

Filling

    2 tablespoons butter, melted
    3 tablespoon sugar
    2 teaspoons ground cinnamon

Topping

    ½ cup powdered sugar

In a mixing bowl, stir together the cherries, raisins, and orange juice. Cover with plastic and set aside, stirring occasionally.

Put the warm water in a large mixing bowl and sprinkle the yeast on top.

Warm the milk to about 110°F (do not boil). Pour the warm milk into a large mixing bowl, then stir in 1 teaspoon honey and 1 cup flour. Cover with plastic wrap and let it rise about 30 minutes, or until the mixture is light and bubbly.

By hand, add the fruit mixture, honey, egg, butter, lemon zest, salt, mace, and 2 cups flour. Gradually add the remaining flour until the dough is still soft but easily pulls away from the sides of the bowl. Knead the dough until it is smooth and stretches well. Put a little oil in the mixing bowl and spread it around with your fingers. Place the dough back in the bowl, then turn the dough over to oil both sides. Cover bowl with a towel and let dough rise about 1 hour.

On a lightly floured surface, roll the dough out to make a large oval. Spread the melted butter over the oval, then sprinkle 3 tablespoons sugar and 2 teaspoons cinnamon on the butter.

Fold the dough in half lengthwise, then carefully press the edges together to help the loaf keep its shape. Place dough on a greased (or parchment paper-lined) baking sheet. Cover with a towel and let dough rise for another 45 minutes.

Preheat oven to 375°F. Bake cake for about 25 minutes, or until the crust is slightly golden brown and the inside is no longer doughy. Cool cake on a wire rack. Dust powdered sugar over the top of the cake just before serving.

→SPICE CAKE←

Spice cake originated in Europe, where it is used to celebrate special occasions and holidays. Because it is so simple to make, spice cake was a popular treat in pioneer America.

1 cup sugar
2½ tablespoons butter, at room
   temperature
2 tablespoons molasses
2 cups flour
1 cup buttermilk
1 teaspoon baking soda
1 teaspoon baking powder
1 teaspoon ground cinnamon
1 teaspoon ground cloves
1 teaspoon ground nutmeg
1 cup raisins

Preheat oven to 350°F. Grease and flour a 9 x 13-inch cake pan.

In a large mixing bowl, cream together the sugar and butter. Gradually stir in the remaining ingredients, adding the raisins last.

Spread into the prepared pan and bake for 35 to 40 minutes, or until a toothpick inserted in the center comes out clean.

If you are not planning to frost the cake, sprinkle about ½ cup sugar and 2 tablespoons cinnamon on the cake before baking.

→BOILED RAISIN AND NUT CAKE←

Boiled raisin and nut cake is a traditional British dish. This cake does not contain eggs, milk, or butter, so it can be stored for an extended period of time, making it an ideal dessert for pioneers.

2 cups sugar
2 cups water
½ cup shortening
2 cups raisins
1 grated apple, including peel
2 cups flour
1 teaspoon baking soda
2 teaspoons baking powder
2 cups chopped walnuts or pecans

1 teaspoon ground cinnamon
1 teaspoon ground nutmeg
1 teaspoon ground cloves

Put the first 5 ingredients in a pot and heat to boiling. Allow to boil for 10 minutes, then remove from heat and let cool at least 30 minutes.

Preheat oven to 350°F. To the mixture in the pot, add the flour, baking soda, baking powder, nuts, and spices. Mix thoroughly.

Spread batter in a greased bundt pan. Bake for about 1 hour, or until a toothpick inserted in the center comes out clean. Let cool in the pan at least 15 minutes before removing.

☞ *You should know a man seven years before you stir his fire.*

→SWISS APPLE PIE←

It is believed that the regions now known as Switzerland and Austria were the first to cultivate apples. This particular pie was a favorite of the Swiss, who brought the recipe with them to America.

¼ cup butter
1½ cups flour, sifted
3 tablespoons cold water
2 tablespoons bread crumbs
4 or 5 Granny Smith apples, cored
    and thinly sliced but not peeled
2 eggs
2 egg yolks
2 cups heavy whipping cream
⅔ cup sugar
2 tablespoons butter, melted

Preheat oven to 350°F. In a mixing bowl, cut ¼ cup butter into the flour with 2 butter knives or a pastry blender. Gradually pour in the water and mash the dough with a fork until it is workable.

On a lightly floured surface, roll out the dough to fit a 10-inch pie plate. Place the dough in the pie plate, then trim and flute the edges.

Sprinkle the breadcrumbs over the pie crust. Next, layer the apple slices evenly on the crust, making a nice design. Bake the pie for 5 to 6 minutes.

In a mixing bowl, whisk the eggs and yolks together, then whisk in the cream. Stir in ½ cup sugar until it dissolves. Pour half of the mixture evenly over the apples. Bake for another 30 minutes.

Pour the remaining egg mixture over the apples, then bake another 30 minutes, or until the apples are tender.

Pour the melted butter evenly over the pie and sprinkle with the remaining sugar. Bake 5 more minutes, or until the top is golden brown. Let pie cool for 10 to 15 minutes before serving.

☞ *Don't halloo till you are out of the wood.*

→NEW ENGLAND APPLE PIE←

In 19th-century America, a common practice among the wealthy was to eat apple pie with a slice of cheddar cheese at the end of a meal. This tradition dates back to medieval England. This particular type of pie was made with dried apples when fresh were not available. If using dried apples, simply soak them in water until they are soft again.

> 2 cups flour
> 1 cup shortening or butter, at room
>   temperature
> 1½ teaspoons salt, divided
> ½ cup cold water
> 5 to 6 crisp apples, cored, peeled,
>   and sliced
> ¾ cup sugar
> 1 teaspoon ground cinnamon
> ½ teaspoon ground nutmeg
> 2 tablespoons flour
> 3 tablespoons butter

Preheat oven to 350°F. Cream together the flour, shortening or butter, 1 teaspoon salt, and cold water. Divide the dough into two sections. On a lightly floured surface, roll out each section to make a large circle. Line a 10-inch pie plate with one of the dough circles; save the other for the top of the pie.

In a mixing bowl, combine the apples, sugar, ½ teaspoon salt, cinnamon, nutmeg, and flour. Gently pour the apple mixture into the lined pie plate. Cut the butter into small chunks, then sprinkle them over the apples. Gently place the second dough circle over the apples and cut 4 to 6 slits into the top for ventilation. Seal the crusts together with wet fingers, cut off the extra, and flute the edges.

Bake pie for 30 to 40 minutes, or until a small knife inserted into one of the slits can easily cut through the apples.

☞ *An apple pie without some cheese is like a kiss without a squeeze.*

→PUMPKIN PIE←

Pumpkin pie in a crust, as we know it today, was developed about 50 years after the first permanent European settlement in New England. From the Native Americans, the settlers learned to remove the innards of a pumpkin or winter gourd, then fill it with cream, honey, and spices. The pumpkin or gourd was then buried in hot ashes and roasted out of doors. (For instructions on how to make fresh pumpkin purée, see http://meatlessmealsformeateaters.blogspot.com/2010_10_01_archive.html.)

Crust

- 2 cups flour
- 1 cup shortening or butter, at room temperature
- 1 teaspoon salt
- ½ cup cold water

Filling

- 2 cups pumpkin, cooked and puréed
- 2 cups cream
- 2 eggs, beaten
- ½ cup molasses
- ½ teaspoon salt
- ½ teaspoon ground cinnamon
- ½ teaspoon ground ginger
- ¼ teaspoon ground nutmeg
- ¼ teaspoon ground cloves

Preheat oven to 450°F. In a mixing bowl, cream together the crust ingredients. Roll out the dough and line a pie plate with it. Cut off the excess and flute the edges.

In a large mixing bowl, whisk together the pumpkin, cream, and eggs. When the batter is smooth, stir in the remaining ingredients. Pour the filling into the prepared pie crust.

Bake pie for 10 minutes, then reduce the heat to 325°F and bake another 30 to 35 minutes, or until a toothpick inserted in the center of the pie comes out clean.

☞ *Blessings brighten as they take their flight.*

⇥CHERRY PIE⇤

Cherry pie is the second most popular pie in the United States, after apple pie. Cherry pie and most other fruit-filled pies are typically served à la mode—*with a sweet, creamy topping such as ice cream or whipped cream. This was a custom made popular in the United States around the 1890s.*

> pastry for 2 pie crusts
> ¾ cup sugar
> ½ cup honey
> ½ cup flour
> 6 cups fresh red cherries, pitted
> 2 tablespoons butter

Preheat oven to 425°F. Line a pie plate with one of the prepared pastry crusts.

In a mixing bowl, whisk together the sugar, honey, and flour. Stir in the cherries, then spread in the pastry-lined pie plate. Cut the butter into chunks and sprinkle on top of the cherry mixture.

Cover the pie with the remaining pastry, cut slits in the top for ventilation (in a pattern for presentation), and seal and flute the edges. Cover the edges of the pie crust with foil to be removed during the last 15 minutes of baking. Bake for 35 to 45 minutes, or until the crust is golden brown and cherry juice begins to bubble through the slits. Cool pie for at least 10 minutes before serving.

⇥PEACH COBBLER⇤

Cobblers were invented by early American settlers who were trying to make favorite dishes from their homeland, such as English steamed puddings. These pioneers excelled at improvising and simply used whatever fruit was in season to make delicious, easy cobblers and pies.

Filling

> 5 peaches, peeled and sliced
> 2 tablespoons butter, melted
> ¼ teaspoon ground cinnamon
> ⅛ teaspoon ground nutmeg
> 1 tablespoon cornstarch
> ½ cup water

Biscuit Crust and Topping

1 cup milk
1 cup sugar
1 cup flour
1½ teaspoons baking powder
⅛ teaspoon salt
⅓ cup butter, melted
1 teaspoon ground cinnamon
¼ teaspoon ground nutmeg

Preheat oven to 350°F. In a small bowl, dissolve the cornstarch in the water and set aside. In a large mixing bowl, combine the remaining ingredients for the filling. Gently fold the cornstarch and water mixture into the peaches, then set aside.

For the biscuit topping, in another large mixing bowl, whisk together the milk, sugar, flour, baking powder, and salt until smooth.

Spread the melted butter in a 9 x 13-inch baking dish. Pour the batter over the melted butter. Spoon the peaches onto the batter, then sprinkle the top with cinnamon and nutmeg. Bake cobbler for 50 minutes to 1 hour.

→APPLE BROWN BETTY←

This dessert was a common treat among 19th-century American settlers. Its modern cousin is apple crisp.

5 apples, cored and sliced
1 cup breadcrumbs
½ cup sugar
3 tablespoons butter, melted
¼ cup orange juice
1 teaspoon orange peel, grated
1 teaspoon cinnamon
whipped cream or ice cream

Preheat oven to 375°F. Layer half of the apples in a buttered pie plate. In a mixing bowl, stir together the remaining ingredients except the rest of the apples, then spread half of that mixture on top of the apple layer.

Next, make another layer with the rest of the apple slices. Then cover evenly with the rest of the breadcrumb mixture.

Bake for about 45 minutes, or until the top is golden brown and the apples are soft. Serve with whipped cream or ice cream.

→APPLE STRUDEL←

Apple strudel was first mentioned in writing in 17ᵗʰ-century Austria, though this filled pastry may have its origins in the Middle East. According to wikipedia.org, strudel *is a German word that comes from the Middle High German word for "whirlpool" or "eddy." The trick to making delicious strudel is getting the dough as thin as possible before adding the filling.*

> 1½ cups flour
> 1 egg
> ¼ teaspoon salt
> 1 heaping tablespoon lard (may
>   substitute vegetable shortening)
> ⅓ cup lukewarm water
> 4 pounds apples
> ¼ cup butter
> 1 cup breadcrumbs
> ½ teaspoon grated lemon rind
> raisins (optional)
> powdered sugar

In a large bowl, combine the flour, egg, salt, and lard or shortening. Add enough water to make a soft dough, then beat until air bubbles form in dough. Cover with a warm towel and place in a warm place for 30 minutes.

In the meantime, peel and slice apples as for pie. Melt butter in a frying pan and add breadcrumbs. Stir constantly until crumbs are lightly browned, then remove from pan.

Preheat oven to 350°F. Spray or grease a 9 x 13-inch baking pan.

Spread a tablecloth on the table and sprinkle lightly with flour. With a rolling pin, roll dough lightly on tablecloth until it is about ½ inch thick. Starting in the center, put hands under the dough and then pull and stretch gently. (Do not poke holes in the dough with your fingers.) Work around the table until the dough is paper thin.

Spread browned breadcrumbs on the dough, then cover with a thin layer of apples. Sprinkle on sugar to taste, then dot with butter. Sprinkle with raisins, lemon rind, and cinnamon.

Take one end of the tablecloth and hold it up so that the dough starts rolling. Once the strudel is rolled, form it into a horseshoe shape. Then put your hand under the tablecloth and flip the strudel into the greased pan.

Bake for 50 to 60 minutes. Sprinkle apple strudel with powdered sugar, then slice and serve.

⁺APPLE FRITTERS⁺

The British make apple fritters—apple rings or chunks fried in batter—as an accompaniment to fish and chips. It was probably these fritters that were adapted by the American pioneers. Unlike the British apple fritter, the American variety is made with a heavy batter that contains spices such as nutmeg and cinnamon.

> 2 cups flour
> ¾ teaspoon baking soda
> ½ teaspoon salt
> 2 tablespoons sugar
> ¼ teaspoon nutmeg
> 2 eggs
> 1⅓ cups buttermilk
> 2 tablespoons butter, at room
>   temperature
> 2 cups diced apples
> 2 quarts cooking oil
> powdered sugar

Sift and measure flour, then sift again with baking soda, salt, sugar, and nutmeg.

Beat eggs well. Add milk and melted shortening; beat until smooth. Fold in apples.

Heat oil in a deep fryer or a heavy-bottomed deep pot or skillet. Oil is ready when it reaches 375°F, or when a cube of bread dropped in the oil is browned in 60 seconds.

In small batches, drop batter by spoonfuls into oil and cook, turning frequently, until fritters are golden brown. Drain fritters on paper towels and dust with powdered sugar.

☞ *One year's seeding makes seven years weeding.*

→APPLE DUMPLINGS←

For hundreds of years, dumplings have been eaten in many different countries and cultures. But according to yum.com, "The apple dumpling is a traditional dessert native to the Pennsylvanian Amish who eat them for breakfast." Many different types of dumplings are popular in the southern United States, including apple, strawberry, ham, chicken, and turkey.

Dumplings

1 pastry for a double-crust pie
  (biscuit dough or shortcake
  dough may be substituted)
6 large, tart apples, peeled, cored,
  and sliced
¾ cup brown sugar
1 teaspoon cinnamon
½ teaspoon nutmeg

Cooking Syrup

3 cups water
2 cups sugar
1 teaspoon vanilla
½ cup (1 stick) butter

Milk Sauce

2 cups milk
½ cup sugar
1½ teaspoons vanilla
dash of nutmeg

Preheat oven to 400°F. Spray a 9 x 13-inch baking pan with cooking spray.

Sprinkle cinnamon, nutmeg, and brown sugar over sliced apples, then toss to coat.

Roll pie crust out to form a large triangle. Cut into six square pieces. Heap apples in the middle, then gather the edges of the dough up to the top and pinch together. Place dumplings in prepared baking pan.

Combine ingredients for cooking syrup in a saucepan. Boil for 5 minutes or until sugar is dissolved. Carefully pour syrup over dumplings, then bake until apples are done, about 50 minutes.

Dumplings are delicious served hot with whipped cream, ice cream, or milk sauce. To make the milk sauce, combine milk, sugar, flavoring, and nutmeg in a small saucepan, then cook for 5 minutes over medium-low heat, stirring constantly. Pour over dumplings while sauce is still hot.

⁺BEIGNETS⁺

Beignets, *which date back to the Middle Ages, are mouthwatering pieces of fried dough that are dusted in powdered sugar. Islamic influences on Spanish cuisine brought about* bunuelos—*balls of dough fried in fat. The French changed the dough slightly, as well as the shape. In the 18ᵗʰ century, large numbers of French immigrants colonized Louisiana, and since then beignets have been popular there, especially in New Orleans.*

¾ cup warm water
¼ cup sugar
1⅛ teaspoons yeast
1 egg
1⅛ teaspoons salt
½ cup buttermilk
3½ cups flour
2 tablespoons soft butter
oil for frying
1½ cups powdered sugar

In a small bowl, stir together the warm water, sugar, and yeast. Let sit for 10 minutes (it should get foamy).

In a large mixing bowl, beat together the egg, salt, and buttermilk. Stir in the foamy yeast mixture. Add 2 cups of flour; combine well. Begin to stir and knead in the last 1½ cups of flour and the soft butter until all of the flour in the bowl is incorporated into the dough (it will be slightly sticky).

Lift the dough, place a dab of oil in the bowl, and spread the oil on the bottom and sides of the bowl. Place the dough back in the bowl and turn the dough over to oil both sides. Cover dough and let rise for 2 hours.

Put ½ cup powdered sugar in a large ziptop plastic bag; set aside. Fill a large skillet about ¾ inch deep with cooking oil and turn burner to medium high.

On a floured surface, roll out the dough into a large rectangle about ¼ inch thick, then cut into 3- to 4-inch squares.

Carefully drop 4 to 6 dough squares at a time into the hot oil and fry on both sides until golden brown, about 1 minute on each side. Beignets cook very quickly, so watch them carefully.

Allow the beignets to dry on paper towels for about 1 minute. Carefully put the hot beignets in the bag of powdered sugar, seal the bag well, and shake the bag to coat the beignets with sugar. As you continue to fry the beignets in batches, add more powdered sugar to the bag.

→GINGER SNAPS←

German and British immigrants brought their recipes for ginger cookies to America. The Germans usually gravitated toward a softer ginger cookie, while the British usually made the crispier kind, such as ginger snaps and gingerbread men. According to easteuropeanfood.about.com, "The first gingerbread man is credited to Queen Elizabeth I, who knocked the socks off visiting dignitaries by presenting them with one baked in their own likeness."

¾ cup molasses
⅓ cup shortening
⅓ cup brown sugar

1¾ cups flour
¾ teaspoon salt
2 teaspoons ground ginger
¾ teaspoon baking soda

Over medium heat in a small saucepan, bring the molasses to a boil. Remove from heat and set aside to cool.

In a large mixing bowl, cream together the shortening and brown sugar. In another mixing bowl, use a fork to stir together the flour, salt, ginger, and baking soda. Add the flour mixture and molasses to the sugar–shortening mixture; mix well. Cover and refrigerate overnight.

Preheat the oven to 375°F. Place the dough on a lightly floured surface and roll out into a large sheet about ¼ inch thick. Cut shapes into the dough with a cookie cutter and place on a parchment paper-lined cookie sheet. Bake cookies for 10 to 12 minutes. Cool on a wire rack.

☞ *A nod's as good as a wink to a blind horse.*

→GINGERBREAD←

In the 11th century, Crusaders brought ginger to Europe from the Middle East. Over time, as the exotic spice became more affordable, it gained popularity in England, France, Germany, Poland, Holland, and Scandinavia, where it was used to flavor cookies and cakes. Immigrants brought their love for ginger-spiced sweets to America, where today the most popular forms are gingerbread men, gingerbread houses, and ginger cake served with lemon or caramel sauce.

2 cups flour
½ cup sugar
1 teaspoon baking powder
½ teaspoon salt
½ teaspoon baking soda
1 teaspoon ground ginger
¼ teaspoon ground cloves
¼ teaspoon ground cinnamon
1 egg
½ cup buttermilk
½ cup (1 stick) butter, melted
¼ cup molasses

Preheat oven to 350ºF. Grease a 9 x 13-inch baking dish. In a large mixing bowl, sift together all of the dry ingredients. In a separate bowl, whisk together the egg and buttermilk, then stir into the flour mixture. Fold the melted butter and molasses into the batter. Stir until smooth.

Spread into the prepared dish and bake for 20 to 30 minutes, or until a toothpick inserted in the center comes out clean. If desired, serve this gingerbread with caramel sauce (recipe follows) and whipped cream.

→CARAMEL SAUCE←

1 cup milk
½ cup sugar
½ cup honey
⅓ cup butter or margarine
2 tablespoons cornstarch
½ teaspoon vanilla
pinch of salt

Whisk all of the ingredients together in a large skillet. Boil for 3 to 5 minutes, stirring constantly. Serve hot over cake.

→MOLASSES COOKIES←

Molasses is the thick, dark brown, uncrystallized juice obtained from sugar during the refining process. American colonists, and later the pioneers, commonly used molasses to sweeten baked goods and drinks. The molasses cookie is evidence of the liquid sweetener's popularity.

¾ cup molasses
½ cup butter
1 egg
½ cup sugar
½ cup milk
2¾ cups flour
4 teaspoons baking powder
½ teaspoon baking soda
½ teaspoon ground cinnamon
½ teaspoon ground ginger
½ teaspoon salt

Preheat oven to 325°F. Line 2 cookie sheets with parchment paper.

Melt the butter and stir in the molasses. In a large bowl, cream together the egg, sugar, and milk. Stir in the molasses mixture.

In a separate bowl, whisk together all of the dry ingredients. Gradually stir the dry mixture into the wet mixture until the dough is smooth.

Drop dough by the spoonful onto the prepared cookie sheets. Bake for 10 to 12 minutes. Cool cookies on a wire rack.

→HONEY COOKIES←

Honey cookies were brought to America by Eastern European immigrants. The cookies can be baked with almonds and/or raisins pressed into the top before baking, or decorated after baking with plain white icing.

1 cup honey
⅓ cup butter
¼ teaspoon ground cloves
1 teaspoon cinnamon
2 eggs
2¼ cups flour
1 teaspoon baking soda
⅓ teaspoon salt

In a small saucepan over medium heat, warm the honey. Stir in the butter, cinnamon, and cloves. Stir constantly until the butter melts and the ingredients are well combined. Remove from heat and let cool.

Preheat oven to 375°F. In a large mixing bowl, whisk together the flour, baking soda, and salt. Whisk the eggs into the cooled honey mixture, then stir in the flour a little at a time, mixing well after each addition.

Drop the dough by spoonfuls onto a parchment paper-lined cookie sheet. Bake for 10 to 13 minutes, or until the cookies are slightly golden brown and set in the center.

→OATMEAL RAISIN COOKIES←

Oatmeal cakes were popular in Scotland and England. By the 19th century, the cakes had evolved into oatmeal cookies, a popular American tradition.

1 cup flour
1 teaspoon baking powder
½ teaspoon baking soda
½ teaspoon salt
2 tablespoons butter, at room temperature
1 cup brown sugar
¼ cup applesauce
1 egg
1 teaspoon vanilla
1⅓ cup oats
½ cup raisins

Preheat oven to 375°F. Line 2 cookie sheets with parchment paper.

In a large mixing bowl, whisk together the flour, baking powder, baking soda, and salt.

In another mixing bowl, cream together the butter and brown sugar until smooth. Stir in the applesauce, egg, and vanilla, combining thoroughly. Mix in the flour, then the oats and raisins.

Drop dough by the spoonful, about 2 inches apart, onto the prepared cookie sheets. Bake for 10 to 12 minutes. Cool cookies on wire racks.

☞ *A stitch in time saves nine.*

⟶PLUM PUDDING⟵

Plum pudding can be traced back to medieval times in England, and English immigrants eventually brought the dish to America. Plum pudding is traditionally served at Christmastime.

½ cup finely chopped raisins
½ cup finely chopped suet
1½ cups flour
½ cup molasses
½ teaspoon ground mace
½ teaspoon ground nutmeg
½ teaspoon ground ginger
½ cup buttermilk
3 eggs, well beaten
powdered sugar

In a large mixing bowl, stir all ingredients together until the batter is mostly smooth. Spread the batter into a 1-quart pudding mold. Cover the mold tightly and place on a rack in a deep pot. Put enough water in the pot to reach halfway up the mold. Steam for 4 hours, adding more water when necessary.

When pudding is done, turn it out of the mold and sprinkle with powdered sugar. Serve warm.

⟶RICE CUSTARD PUDDING⟵

In the United States, most rice pudding recipes were handed down from early European immigrants, then adapted for modern cooking methods. The earliest rice puddings in England date from the Tudor period and were called "whitepot." At Christmastime in Sweden and Finland, a whole almond is hidden in the rice pudding or porridge, and the person who eats the almond is expected to have good luck the following year, while in Norway, Denmark, and Iceland, the person who eats the almond receives a gift (see wikipedia.org/wiki/Rice_pudding). This tradition has been handed down to many Americans of Scandinavian descent.

¼ cup rice
3 eggs
1 quart milk
½ cup sugar
½ cup raisins
1 teaspoon vanilla

Steam the rice in a small, covered pot. Add beaten eggs, milk, sugar, and raisins; mix thoroughly. Stir in vanilla.

Pour in a 1½-quart casserole dish and bake at 325°F for 50 to 60 minutes, or until a custard forms.

⤳BAKED INDIAN PUDDING⤳

Developed by New England colonists, this dish probably had nothing to do with Native Americans. Rather, colonists had a tendency to call anything "indian" that contained corn. This pudding is delicious served with whipped cream or vanilla ice cream.

> 3 cups milk
> ¼ cup molasses
> 3 tablespoons cornmeal
> 1 egg
> ½ cup sugar
> ½ teaspoon salt
> ½ teaspoon ginger
> ½ teaspoon cinnamon
> ½ cup cold milk
> ½ stick butter

Preheat oven to 325°F. Scald 3 cups milk. Add molasses and cornmeal, then cook until thick. Remove pan from heat.

Stir together the egg, sugar, salt, ginger, and cinnamon. Add to milk mixture. Pour into a greased 1½-quart casserole dish. Bake for 30 minutes.

Add ½ cup cold milk and butter. Continue baking for about 1 hour, or until pudding is firm.

☞ *From toil he wins his spirits light;*
From busy day the peaceful night;
Rich, from the very want of wealth,
In heaven's best treasures, peace and health.

THOMAS GRAY

→BUTTERMILK SUET PUDDING WITH BUTTER SAUCE←

Traditional suet pudding comes from England and is made from chopped beef suet and flour. Often, ingredients such as raisins, nuts, and spices are added. Suet pudding is steamed, sometimes in a cloth. This recipe contains buttermilk, which keeps the pudding moist, and is steamed in a coffee can or pudding mold.

Pudding

1 pound suet, chopped fine
1 pound seedless raisins
1 cup sugar
1 cup molasses
1 egg
½ teaspoon ground cinnamon
½ teaspoon ground nutmeg
½ teaspoon ground allspice
1 cup buttermilk
2 cups flour
½ teaspoon salt
1 teaspoon baking soda
2 teaspoons baking powder
1 teaspoon vanilla

Butter Sauce

⅔ cup sugar
1½ tablespoons cornstarch
1 cup water
¼ cup butter
½ teaspoon nutmeg
¼ teaspoon cinnamon
1 teaspoon vanilla

Mix flour with baking soda, baking powder, spices, suet, salt, and sugar. Stir molasses, buttermilk, and vanilla into dry ingredients. Add raisins and stir until thoroughly combined.

Spoon mixture into two greased 1-pound coffee cans or one greased 2-quart pudding mold. Cover with aluminum foil that has been sprayed with cooking spray.

Place cans or mold on a rack in a large pot. Add enough boiling water to come halfway up the side of the cans or mold. Place lid on the pot and steam pudding for 3 hours, or until a toothpick inserted in the center comes out clean.

Remove cans or mold from pot. Let pudding stand about 10 minutes. With a knife, loosen pudding around edge of cans or mold, then turn out.

To make the sauce, combine sugar and cornstarch in small saucepan. Stir in water. Cook over medium heat until thick and bubbly, stirring constantly. Add butter, vanilla, and spices; mix thoroughly.

Serve pudding warm with hot butter sauce.

ROLY PUDDING

Jam roly-poly is a traditional British dessert probably invented in the early 1800s. The pudding is rolled flat, then spread with jam and rolled up. According to historicalfoods.com, "Jam roly-poly is a Victorian dessert ('roly-poly' is British slang for anything round) which was also known as shirt-sleeve pudding, because it was often steamed or boiled in an old shirt-sleeve, a replacement muslin cloth for the poor." Other nicknames of the pudding are "dead-man's arm" and "dead man's leg."

2 cups sifted flour
½ teaspoon salt
4 teaspoons baking powder
¼ cup (½ stick) butter
¾ cup milk

Mix dry ingredients in a medium-size bowl. Mix in shortening with fingers. Add milk to make a soft dough.

Gently roll or pat out dough to create oblong shapes that are ½ inch thick. Spread generously with jam of any kind, then roll like a jelly roll.

Place rolled puddings on a cloth in a steamer over boiling water. (The cloth will prevent the puddings from becoming soaked with water.) Cover pan tightly and steam for at least 30 minutes.

Cut pudding in slices. Serve with whipped cream, ice cream, or fruit sauce.

✦POOR MAN'S SUET PUDDING✦

Pioneers often used suet to make pastries, puddings, and mincemeat. Suet is the hard, white fat from the kidneys or loins of cattle, sheep, and other animals.

Pudding

    1½ cups suet
    pinch salt
    4 cups flour
    1 cup raisins
    cold water

Sauce

    3 tablespoons sugar
    ¼ cup (½ stick) butter, melted
    1 tablespoon flour
    nutmeg, to taste

Combine pudding ingredients. Tie in cloth bag and boil in water for 3 hours. Combine sauce ingredients. Add water to desired thickness, then add nutmeg. Serve sauce hot over hot pudding.

✦CARROT PUDDING✦

Carrot pudding is a traditional dish in many countries around the world. It has been served in Ireland since the 1700s, and Irish immigrants probably brought the dish to America. Carrot pudding can be served as a savory pudding (a side dish) or a dessert, as below.

    1 cup grated carrots
    1 cup breadcrumbs
    1 cup flour
    2 cups raisins
    1 cup currants
    1½ cups brown sugar
    ¾ cup buttermilk or sour milk
    1 cup fine suet (1 cup [2 sticks]
        butter may be substituted)
    3 eggs, well beaten
    1 teaspoon baking soda
    3 teaspoons baking powder
    1 teaspoon ground cinnamon
    ½ teaspoon ground nutmeg
    ¼ teaspoon ground cloves
    ½ teaspoon salt

In a large bowl, mix all ingredients thoroughly. Butter the top pan of a double boiler, then put the pudding in the top pan. Pour water in the bottom pan of the double boiler until it reaches about two inches up the sides.

Cook pudding for 3½ hours in the double boiler, regularly replacing the water as it boils down. (Do not put too much water in the pan or the pudding will rise.)

Serve pudding warm, topped with whipped cream or ice cream.

→BREAD PUDDING←

Bread pudding has very old culinary roots. It was made with stale bread by cooks who did not want to waste food, which was viewed as a sin of ingratitude. Pioneer cooks were also experts at improvising and making do, even when ingredients were less than perfect tasting.

> 2 eggs
> 1 cup sugar
> 3 cups milk
> 1 cup cream
> 1 teaspoon vanilla

½ cup (1 stick) butter
8 slices of stale bread
cinnamon

Preheat oven to 350°F. In a large mixing bowl, beat together the eggs, sugar, milk, cream, and vanilla until smooth. Tear the bread into pieces and place them in the wet mixture.

Pour the mixture into a baking dish. Cut the butter into chunks and sprinkle over the top. Dust the top of the pudding with cinnamon. Bake for about 1 hour or until the pudding is no longer sticky.

*Beware of an oak,
it draws the stroke;
avoid an ash,
it counts the flash;
creep under the thorn,
it can save you from harm.*

→BACHELOR PUDDING←

Bachelor pudding probably originated in England, and it became popular in America in the 1800s. A recipe for the pudding was published in 1861 in The Book of Household Management, *with a note indicating that the dish was "seasonable from August to March."*

> 2 cups chopped apples
> 2 cups soft breadcrumbs
> 1 cup dried raisins (currants may be substituted)
> ½ cup sugar
> ½ cup finely diced candied lemon peel
> 1 egg
> 1½ tablespoons butter
> dash of nutmeg

Mix together apples, breadcrumbs, raisins, sugar, nutmeg, and lemon peel. Add beaten egg, melted butter, and nutmeg. Stir until well blended.

Spoon batter into a greased pudding mold. Then place mold on a rack in a large pot with water in it. Cover pot and steam pudding for 2 hours, replenishing water as necessary.

Serve pudding with whipped cream or ice cream.

→VANILLA SAUCE←

This sauce is delicious served hot on mincemeat pie, steamed puddings, or fruit cobblers.

> ½ cup sugar
> 1 tablespoon cornstarch
> 1 cup boiling water
> 2 tablespoons butter
> 1½ teaspoons vanilla extract
> dash salt

Combine sugar and cornstarch in a small saucepan. Stir in 1 cup boiling water. Simmer for 5 minutes, stirring constantly.

Stir in butter, vanilla extract, and salt; blend well. Serve hot or cold over dessert of choice.

☞ *A bad penny always turns up.*

Candies and
Drinks

The Old Pioneers

Oh, I love to read the story
Of the grand old pioneer,
Living in his little cabin
On the wild, wierd [sic] frontier.

Far away from native homestead
By childhood's memories blest,
When this goodly land of ours
Was a wilderness, out west.

Oh, I fancy now I see him
Sitting in his cabin door,
In the shadows of the evening,
When the hard day's work is o'er.

In the forest dark and gloomy,
Clustering all around his home,
Undergrown with briars and bushes
Where the bear and panther roam.

And the prowling wolf in shyness,
For the darkness lies in wait,
Whilst he sits alone in silence
Dreaming of his native state.

All unconscious of the darkness,
And the dangers lurking nigh,
Until wakened from his musings
By the panther's fearful cry;

Borne upon the night winds chilly,
Heard above the rustling leaves,
Then he blinds the little windows
Just beneath the clapboard eaves.

Piles the rough wood in the corner
On the heavy puncheon floor,
Draws the string in through the latchet,
Fastens well the oaken door.

Wife and children all around him,
Sleeps he 'til the morning sun,
Safe as any king in palace
With his faithful dog and gun.

Honest hands by toiling hardened,
Honest hearts that knew no fears.
Oh, I love to hear the story
Of the grand old pioneers.

H. T. Cotton, 1887

⇥CARAMELS⇤

Boiling milk, fat, and sugar to make caramel candy has been an American tradition since sugar became readily available in the early colonies.

> ¾ cup heavy whipping cream
> ½ cup sugar
> ½ cup brown sugar, firmly packed
> 1 teaspoon salt
> 1 teaspoon vanilla

Butter an 8-inch square baking dish. In a large skillet over medium-high heat, stir together the cream, sugars, and salt. Stir constantly until the mixture begins to boil. Let it boil, without stirring, until it reaches 245ºF degrees (use a candy thermometer).

Remove from heat and stir in the vanilla. Pour into the prepared baking dish and let the caramel cool overnight. Using a sharp knife, cut the caramel into squares and wrap in wax paper.

☞ *If the shoe fits, wear it.*

⇥ENGLISH TOFFEE⇤

Toffee originated in northern England and became popular in the 1800s. When the recipe for this simple candy spread to North America, the treat kept its English name. Many pioneers enjoyed making English toffee.

> 2 cups butter
> 2 cups sugar
> ¼ teaspoon salt

Line a cookie sheet with parchment paper. In a large skillet over medium-high heat, stir together all the ingredients. Bring the mixture to a boil and stir occasionally until it reaches 285ºF (use a candy thermometer).

Pour the liquid candy onto the prepared sheet. Refrigerate at least two hours, then break into pieces.

☞ *The difficult is done at once, the impossible takes a little longer.*

⊹FUDGE DELIGHT⊹

Scottish tablet is a very sweet candy made of sugar, butter, and condensed milk. Americans added cocoa to the candy, and the concoction was called "fudge."

¼ cup (½ stick) unsalted butter
6 ounces semisweet chocolate chips
⅓ cup evaporated milk
1-pound package powdered sugar
1 teaspoon vanilla
pinch of salt
½ cup chopped walnuts (optional)
1 cup miniature marshmallows

Butter an 8-inch square pan. In a saucepan, heat the butter, chocolate chips, and milk over medium heat, stirring constantly until smooth.

Pour mixture into a large bowl. Beat in powdered sugar, vanilla, and salt. Fold in the chopped walnuts and miniature marshmallows. Pour into prepared square pan.

Let sit for an hour, then cut into 36 pieces. Fudge is best when refrigerated.

⊹MOLASSES CANDY⊹

Molasses candy was a popular treat among pioneers.

1 cup molasses
½ cup brown sugar, firmly packed
1½ tablespoons butter
½ tablespoon vinegar

Butter a small pan and set aside. In a heavy skillet, combine the molasses, brown sugar, and butter. Cook over medium-high heat, stirring frequently, until the liquid reaches 250°F. Stir in the vinegar and continue cooking until it reaches 260°F (use a candy thermometer).

Pour into the prepared pan and use a knife to mark 1-inch squares in the candy while it is still warm. Break or cut the candy after it is completely cooled.

☞ *Variety is the spice of life.*

→SALTWATER TAFFY←

The American candy called taffy is derived from its British cousin, toffee. Taffy became extremely popular in the 1800s, with parties often centered around making it. These parties were referred to as candy pulls or taffy pulls.

　1 pound sugar
　½ teaspoon cornstarch
　1 pound corn syrup
　1 tablespoon butter
　1 cup water
　½ teaspoon salt

In a large kettle over medium-high heat, stir together all ingredients except the salt. Stir frequently. Once the taffy reaches 256ºF, stir in the salt.

Pour the hot taffy onto a buttered slab and let sit until it is cool enough to handle. Pull taffy on a hook or with a pulling partner for about 10 minutes, or until the taffy takes on a glossy texture.

Serve taffy on sticks, or cut into squares and wrap each in a small piece of wax paper.

→POPCORN BALLS←

According to Andrew F. Smith, popcorn balls were among the most popular confections in the late 1800s and early 1900s. Smith says that though references to popcorn balls appeared as early as the 1840s, the first recipe was published in 1861 in the Housekeepers Encyclopedia. *(see Andrew F. Smith,* Popped Culture: A Social History of Popcorn in America *[University of South Carolina Press, 1997]).*

　12 cups popped popcorn
　4 tablespoons butter
　½ cup sugar
　1 cup molasses

Place popcorn in a large bowl. Melt butter in a heavy saucepan. Add sugar and molasses, and bring mixture to a boil. Reduce heat and boil gently for 3 to 5 minutes, without stirring, until it reaches the hard-crack stage or 290ºF.

Pour the caramel over the popcorn in a thin stream, stirring with a wooden spoon. Let sit for 1 to 2 minutes, or until popcorn is cool enough to handle. With lightly buttered hands, form the popcorn into balls.

✦HONEY ROOT BEER✦

Root beer is known as one of the "small beers" that originated in colonial America. Sarsaparilla beer, birch beer, and ginger beer were also included in the category of "small beers," which were commonly made with herbs, barks, and roots.

1 quart warm water
1⅓ cups honey
¾ ounce root beer extract
⅛ teaspoon yeast

Pour ½ quart of warm water into a liter container. Stir in the honey, root beer extract, and yeast. Add the remaining ½ quart warm water. Carefully rotate the jug to mix the ingredients, then tightly cap it. Lay the jug on its side (you may want to put a towel around it in case it leaks), and let it set out at room temperature for about 24 hours. Refrigerate the root beer and serve it cold.

☞ *The first wealth is health.*

RALPH WALDO EMERSON

✦LEMONADE✦

Lemons, which originated in the Middle East and Egypt, were first grown in America in the 1700s, in the regions now known as Florida and California. The pioneers loved the sweet-tart taste of lemonade.

8 cups water
1½ cups lemon juice
1½ cups sugar

Combine all ingredients in a large pitcher, stirring until the sugar is dissolved. Adjust the sugar/water ratio if the lemons are too bitter.

✦HONEY LEMONADE✦

Honey was a common sweetener among the pioneers. It was free if found in the wild, but many pioneers kept their own bees in order to have a regular supply of honey.

1 cup honey
1 cup hot water

juice from 8 lemons
8 cups cold water

In a large pitcher, combine the honey and hot water. Next, stir in the lemon juice and cold water. Serve lemonade cold or over ice.

→WASSAIL←

Wassail comes from British immigrants and was often enjoyed during winter holidays.

1 gallon apple cider
½ gallon orange juice
5 cups water
4 tablespoons brown sugar
2 cinnamon sticks
5 whole cloves

In a large pot, combine all the ingredients. Heat the mixture on the stove until the desired temperature is reached.

☞ *Willful waste makes woeful want.*

→HOT CHOCOLATE←

According to wikipedia.org, "The first chocolate beverage is believed to have been created by the Mayan peoples around 2,000 years ago, and a cocoa beverage was an essential part of Aztec culture by 1400 AD. The beverage became popular in Europe after being introduced from Mexico." Cocoa was brought to North America by the Dutch in the 1600s. It was sold in restaurants and stores in the States beginning in the mid 1700s.

¼ cup unsweetened cocoa
¼ cup honey
2 cups hot water
2 cups hot milk
½ teaspoon vanilla

Warm the water and milk in a saucepan, then whisk in the remaining ingredients. Serve hot.

→SAGE TEA←

Sage tea is made with garden sage, not sagebrush. American pioneers used tea made from sage leaves to treat sore throats, coughs, and fevers, as well as rheumatism and digestive problems. According to herbwisdom.com, sage tea is also helpful in the treatment of typhoid fever, liver complaints, kidney troubles, head colds, measles, joint pain, lethargy, palsy, and headaches.

> garden sage leaves
> cream
> sugar

Brew the sage leaves in very hot water. Add cream and sugar to taste.

→BRIGHAM TEA←

Mormon pioneers brewed a tea with leaves from the plant Ephedra viridis, *which was commonly known as joint fir, squaw tea, desert tea, miner's tea, or Mexican tea. Now, the plant is usually referred to as Brigham tea or Mormon tea. The tea was often used to treat allergies, colds, coughs, and many other maladies. Undoubtedly, Brigham tea was effective in treating respiratory illnesses; pharmacologists have determined that the plant contains ephedrine and pseudophedrine, ingredients in many modern cold medicines. (For more information, see herballegacy.com.)*

> Brigham tea leaves
> sugar or honey
> milk

Steep the leaves in hot water. If treating a respiratory illness, serve the tea without milk, with sugar or honey to taste.

☞ *Good health and good sense are two of life's greatest blessings.*

Food Preservation

The Gathering Clouds

When storm clouds gather round us
Do trembles come from fear?
Is our faith badly shaken
For all that we hold dear?
Or can we hold our heads up
With hearts and minds steadfast
Facing such perils bravely
Until the trails are past?
This world is full of heartache
For this we know is true
We can't solve all our problems
Nor know just what to do
We must first see the reason
For badness so,
Love with strong faith for man's maker
And promised things will show
This brings contentment
No fear can wipe away
And our faith never leaves us

Who cares what men may say
So lets pull together
To stay on God's right way
Then we'll know hope's fulfillment
That joyous happy day.

AUTHOR UNKNOWN

→BEEF JERKY←

Beef jerky was a common trail food among the pioneers. Native Americans and trappers often used the dried meat as a bartering tool at trading posts. Venison or buffalo can easily be substituted for beef in this recipe.

  2 pounds lean steak
  ½ cup Worcestershire sauce
  ½ cup soy sauce
  3 tablespoons honey
  2 teaspoons pepper
  2 teaspoons onion powder
  1 teaspoon liquid smoke
  1 teaspoon salt

Cut the meat into very thin strips, or have the butcher do this for you. If cutting the meat yourself, you may want to freeze it for a few hours first to make it easier to cut.

Put the meat and all other ingredients in a large, zip-top plastic bag. Seal the bag, then mix the ingredients together with your hands. Place the bag in the refrigerator for 5 to 7 hours to allow the flavors to marry.

Place the strips of meat in a food dehydrator and dehydrate for about 12 hours at 200ºF to 250ºF, following the manufacturer's directions for the dehydrator.

→DRIED APPLES←

Apples were probably the most commonly dried fruit among the pioneers. Reconstituted dried apple slices can be used in place of fresh apple slices in any cake or bread recipe. The following method may be used for many other types of fruit.

  apple slices
  lemon, lime, or orange juice

Cut the apples into thin slices (whether or not you peel the apple is up to you). To prevent browning, lightly dip the slices in lemon, lime, or orange juice. Place the apple slices in a single layer on dehydrator screens, then dehydrate for 8 to 12 hours at 110ºF to 150ºF.

☞ *Civility costs nothing.*

⇥CANDIED FRUIT⇤

Pioneers used candied fruit in many cakes, cookies, and breads. Candying fruit was a way to enjoy fruit during the long winter months. Fruits that may be candied include apricots, peaches, pineapples, plums, cherries, apples, pears, mangoes, figs, grapes, and blueberries. Ginger, lemon peel, orange peel, and grapefruit peel may also be candied.

    2½ cups sugar
    1 cup water
    1 cup fruit

Cut the fruit into chunks. (Blueberries may be candied whole.) In a saucepan, combine the water and 2 cups sugar. Cook over medium heat, stirring frequently, until the soft-ball stage is reached.

Stir in the fruit chunks and cook the fruit until the syrup is clear. Remove saucepan from heat and let the fruit sit in the syrup overnight.

Drain the fruit very well. Place the remaining ½ cup sugar in a small bowl and roll each piece of fruit in the sugar. Place fruit pieces in a single layer on a dehydrator screen and dehydrate at 250°F until the surface of the fruit is very firm. (Alternately, you may dry the fruit on a cookie sheet in the oven.) Check the fruit frequently while it is drying to make sure it does not become too hard.

⇥BLACKBERRY JAM⇤

Blackberries grow wild in almost every state. Pioneers commonly gathered wild blackberries for snacking, pies, cobblers, jams, and jellies.

    2 pounds crushed blackberries
    2 pounds sugar
    ¼ cup lemon juice

Combine ingredients in a large saucepan. Stir frequently and heat on medium to medium-high heat until the mixture boils. Reduce heat and continue cooking until the desired consistency is reached.

Pour into sterilized jars. Process for about 5 minutes in a boiling water bath. Let sit for at least 24 hours before checking the seal.

→STRAWBERRY PRESERVES←

"Wife, into the garden and set me a plot
With strawberry roots, the best to be got
Such growing abroad among thorns in the wood,
Well chosen and picked, prove excellent good."
—*Tusser, 1557*

6 pints strawberries
10 cups sugar
3 cups lemon juice

Wash and hull the berries. In a large mixing bowl, stir the sugar and strawberries together and let sit for 4 to 5 hours.

Transfer berries to a pot and cook over medium heat, stirring frequently. When the mixture starts to boil, add the lemon juice. Cook until berries are clear and liquid has thickened.

Pour the mixture into a shallow pan and let it cool overnight. Pour into about 8 hot, sterilized half-pint jars. Process for about 5 minutes in a boiling water bath. Let jars sit for at least 24 hours before checking the seal.

→BOTTLED FRUIT←

Pioneers often bottled fruit in the summer and fall to preserve it for the winter. This kind of bottling method works best with cherries, peaches, apricots, plums, and pears.

5 pounds fruit, peeled and sliced
8 cups sugar (or white grape juice)
5 cups water

Fill jars with the prepared fruit. In a pot, stir the sugar and water and heat to boiling. Remove from heat, then pour the hot syrup over the fruit to fill the jars.

Place the lids on the jars and then put the jars in a water bath canner. Cover the jars with warm water, then heat slowly for about 25 to 30 minutes. Remove jars from the bath, then let sit for at least 24 hours before testing the seal.

☞ *Health lies in labor, and there is no royal road to it but through toil.*

Wendell Phillips

→SPICED PEACHES←

These peaches taste delicious in pies or cobblers, or eaten by themselves or with whipped cream or ice cream on top.

> 2 dozen peaches
> 8 cups sugar (or white grape juice)
> 2½ cups apple cider vinegar
> 4 cinnamon sticks
> 4 teaspoons whole cloves
> 1½ cups water

Peel peaches and cut them in half, then remove the pits. If desired, cut peaches into quarters or slices.

In a large pot, combine the sugar, water, and vinegar. Wrap the cinnamon sticks and cloves in a cheesecloth and add to the pot. Bring the syrup to a boil, cover, and let boil for 5 minutes. Remove the lid and let boil 5 more minutes.

Stir in the peaches, then bring to a boil again and simmer for 10 minutes. Remove the wrapped spices.

Fill each jar to about ¼ inch from the top with the spiced peaches. Wipe any excess liquid off of the brim of each jar. Place a lid on each jar.

Process peaches in a boiling water bath with at least 1 inch of water over the jars for about 10 minutes. Let jars sit for 24 hours before checking the seal.

→DRIED STRING BEANS←

Pioneers often preserved green beans by tying them in a row on a long string and hanging them to dry for a few weeks, much like dried herbs and flowers. After the green beans were dried, they could be added to soup, where the broth would reconstitute them, or soaked in water until they were tender again, then cooked as needed.

☞ *It is not spring until you can plant your foot upon twelve daisies.*

→DILL PICKLES←

During the 1400s, many sailors suffered from scurvy. The ship stocker for the Nina, *the* Pinta, *and the* Santa Maria *(the ships under Christopher Columbus' direction in 1492 when he discovered the Americas) stocked a large amount of pickles for the voyage. Unbeknown to the stocker, this decision saved the sailors from contracting scurvy, thanks to the vitamin C in the pickles.*

> 3 quarts water
> 1 quart apple cider vinegar
> 1 cup pickling salt
> fresh dill sprigs
> pickling cucumbers

Put a sprig of dill in the bottom of each jar, then fill jars with cucumbers. Top each jar with another sprig of dill.

In a pot, combine the water, vinegar, and salt. Bring to a boil.

Pour the hot brine into the jars to fill them. Put the lids on the jars. Process in a boiling water bath for at least 5 minutes.

→DRIED HERBS←

These drying directions work for most varieties of herbs.

> herbs of choice, freshly picked

Gather the herbs and and tie them into small bundles. Tie the bundles on a string and hang them upside down in a dry, airy place. (You may want to tie brown paper bags with holes over the herb bundles so they don't get dusty.) Allow the herbs to dry for about 2 weeks, or until they crumble when touched.

Pick the herb leaves off the stems and crush the leaves. Store them in sealable containers.

→CREOLE SEASONING←

This combination of spices is typical in Creole cuisine, which originated in Louisiana. Creole food has strong influences from Louisiana's early settlers, who included Native Americans as well as immigrants from Portugal, France, Spain, India, Greece, and Africa. This Creole seasoning is very versatile and is delicious with beef, poultry, seafood, potatoes, rice, and vegetables.

⅓ cup cayenne pepper
¼ cup plus 1 teaspoon sea salt
2 tablespoons garlic powder
2 tablespoons onion powder
2 tablespoons chili powder
1 tablespoon plus 1 teaspoon
   cracked pepper
1 teaspoon ground cumin

In a bowl, whisk all ingredients together. Store seasoning in an airtight container for up to 6 months.

☞ *Don't go near the water until you learn how to swim.*

Self-Care and
Remedies

The Pioneer

Rouse! brothers, rouse! we've far to travel,
Free as the winds we love to roam,
Far through the prairie, far through the forest,
Over the mountains we'll find a home.
We cannot breathe in crowded cities,
We're strangers to the ways of trade;
We long to feel the grass beneath us,
And ply the hatchet and the spade.
Meadows and hills and ancient woodlands
Offer us pasture, fruit, and corn;
Needing our presence, courting our labor;—
Why should we linger like me forlorn?
We love to hear the ringing rifle,
The smiting axe, the falling tree;—
And though our life be rough and lonely,
If it be honest, what care we?

Fair elbow-room for men to thrive in!
Wide elbow-room for work or play!
If cities follow, tracing our footsteps,
Ever to westward shall point the way!
Rude though our life, it suits our spirit,
And newborn States in future years
Shall own us founders of a nation—
And bless the hardy pioneers.

CHARLES MACKAY (1814–1889)

Some of the pioneers' homemade remedies and self-care recipes are quite useful, while some make us chuckle because of our modern understanding of medicine and science. Please use good judgment and common sense if you decide to try these recipes and remedies. Consult your doctor for modern and effective treatments of wounds and illnesses.

✦HOMEMADE LYE SOAP✦

On a single day, many pioneer households would make enough soap to last the entire year. (Perhaps the chore wasn't their most favorite.) The following type of lye soap was used for everything: washing dishes, washing floors, and washing bodies and hands. Of course, pioneers didn't have canned lye like we do today, so they would make their own lye by pouring water over wood ashes.

 1 cup lard
 ½ cup cold water
 1½ tablespoons lye

Melt the lard. In a small mixing bowl, stir together the water and lye. Pour the solution into the fat. Beat the ingredients together for about 20 minutes with an egg beater. Spread the soap in a cake pan. When the soap has completely solidified, cut it into squares.

✦HOMEMADE LAVENDER SOAP✦

Lavender has been used as a cleansing herb for centuries. The very name lavender *stems from the Latin word* lave, *which means "to clean."*

 2½ cups coconut oil
 3½ cups olive oil
 2½ cups palm oil
 ¼ cup lavender extract
 3 cups water
 1 cup lye

Melt and stir together the oils. In a mixing bowl, combine the water and lye. Pour the solution into the oil mixture, then beat with an egg beater for about 20 minutes. Pour into cake pans. When the soap has completely solidified, cut into squares or rectangles.

⟶HOMEMADE SHAMPOO⟵

In pioneer times, a common gift from a man to his fiancé was a comb, a brush, and a mirror. Typically, a family owned one comb and brush for everyone to share. Most pioneers only washed their hair, using homemade lye soap (see page 173), between once a week and once a month. When they didn't wash their hair, they would often comb oil into it.

> ¼ cup distilled water
> ¼ cup liquid Castile soap
> ½ teaspoon grape seed oil

Mix ingredients together in a bottle. Shake before each use.

⟶HOMEMADE TOOTHBRUSH⟵

For a toothbrush, a pioneer might use a small twig that had been chewed on the end.

> small twig
> small piece of cloth

Wrap the cloth around the end of the twig, then use it to brush your teeth.

⟶HOMEMADE TOOTHPASTE⟵

Pioneers would dip a twig in salt and use it to brush their teeth. Another toothpaste was a mixture of homemade soap, charcoal, and chalk. This is a slightly more modern recipe.

> 6 tablespoons baking soda
> 1 tablespoon vegetable-based
>   glycerin
> 1 tablespoon 3% hydrogen peroxide
> ½ teaspoon mint extract, or to taste
>   (optional)

Stir all ingredients together in a mixing bowl. Spread a dab of this paste on a toothbrush and rub on teeth to clean. Do not ingest this paste; spit it out when teeth are clean.

☞ *He who hesitates is lost.*

→HOMEMADE CANDLES←

Candles were originally made from tallow from cows, sheep, and large game. Later, whale oil was used, as well as beeswax and bayberry wax. Paraffin wax was first used in the mid 1800s. Braided wicks were also invented in the 1800s. Before that, wicks were created by twisting strands of cotton together.

> wax
> wicks
> food coloring (optional)

Melt the wax in a double boiler, and stir in food coloring if using. When the wax is completely melted, take a wick and dip the end into the wax as far as you want the candle to be tall. Hold the wick up for a few moments, letting the dipped wax dry, then dip it again.

Repeat this process until you have reached the desired length and width of the candle. When the wax on the wick has dried completely, cut the wick down to a reasonable length on top of the candle. Repeat until you run out of wax and wicks.

→GRUEL←

Gruel was considered a medicinal food for the ailing. If the sick person wasn't well enough to chew raisins, the raisins were omitted.

> 2 cups water
> ¼ cup oatmeal, cornmeal, or rye
> ⅓ cup raisins
> 1 teaspoon sugar
> ¼ teaspoon salt
> dash of ground nutmeg

In a saucepan over medium heat, boil the water. Stir in the oatmeal, cornmeal, or rye. Boil for 8 to 10 minutes, then stir in the raisins and seasonings.

→HONEY COUGH SYRUP←

Honey has been used medicinally since ancient times. Modern research actually confirms that honey has antibacterial, antiviral, and antifungal properties.

½ cup honey
juice from 1 lemon (no seeds)

Whisk the honey and lemon juice together. Put in a bottle and take by spoonfuls as needed.

→ONION COUGH SYRUP←

Pioneers were on to something when they used onions to make cough syrup. Studies have shown that onions may help to alleviate or prevent sore throats. In fact, onions are a main ingredient in a common remedy for sore throats that is widely used in India today.

sliced onions
honey

Preheat oven to 200°F. On a cookie sheet, spread out the onion slices, then pour honey over them. Bake the onions until they are translucent. Scrape up the syrup and put it in a bottle. To ease a cough, take spoonfuls of the syrup as needed.

→OINTMENT FOR CUTS AND SCRAPES←

For several generations, marigold flowers have been used to treat various ailments, including stomach upset and fever. (Some herbal supplements contain possibly harmful impurities or additives, so check with your pharmacist for details about the particular brand you use, if you intend to ingest marigold orally.) When used regularly, the ointment below speeds the healing of cuts and scrapes.

2 cups lard
handful of marigold blossoms
1 tablespoon glycerin

Melt the lard with the marigold blossoms. Strain to remove the blossoms, then stir in the glycerin. Store this salve in a jar and use as needed.

Miscellaneous Pioneer Remedies

- For a spring tonic, mix anvil dust with cream, or mix molasses and sulfur powder.
- To treat exposure to poison ivy or poison oak, make a solution of Epsom salts and water. Dip a towel in the solution, then hold it over the infected areas.
- To soothe diaper rash or inflamed skin, rub the rash with cream (from cow's or goat's milk), and/or dust the skin with cornstarch.
- To cure hiccups, drink nine sips of water, then walk backwards nine steps. Or while holding your breath, count to 100 backwards.
- To keep ants out of a house, sprinkle cayenne pepper around the walls of the home.
- To cure acne, make a solution of wheat germ and milk, then rub it on the infected area.
- To soothe burns, make a solution of vinegar and water, then soak the burn in the solution until the pain has stopped.
- To soothe an insect bite, cover the bite with wet mud and let the mud dry on the skin.
- For sinus pressure and infections, eat raw garlic cloves and/or raw jalapenos two to three times a day.
- To cure an earache, put a drop of olive oil in each infected ear.
- To get rid of tapeworms, chew on pumpkin seeds in the evening.
- To prevent the mumps, carry in your pocket the chip of a log, then rub it on your jaws and throat every so often.
- To cure fever blisters, kiss a redhead.

⇢AUTHOR BIOGRAPHY⇠

Miriam Barton was born in the Gulf Coast region of Texas and was brought up on Tex-Mex, Cajun, and soul food. As a young adult, she lived in Italy, where she learned that life revolves around food, and that the Italian way is to make meals as delicious as possible. Miriam has spent many years learning the art of creative cooking and has mastered vegetarian cuisine as well as a healthy lifestyle. *The Pioneer Cookbook*: *Recipes for Today's Kitchen* is her first cookbook. Her second cookbook, *Meatless Meals for Meat Eaters,* will be published soon. She also has a healthy desserts cookbook in the works. Miriam, her husband, and their children reside in Centerville, Utah.

INDEX